FILIPINO MARTIAL ARTS
Cabales Serrada Escrima

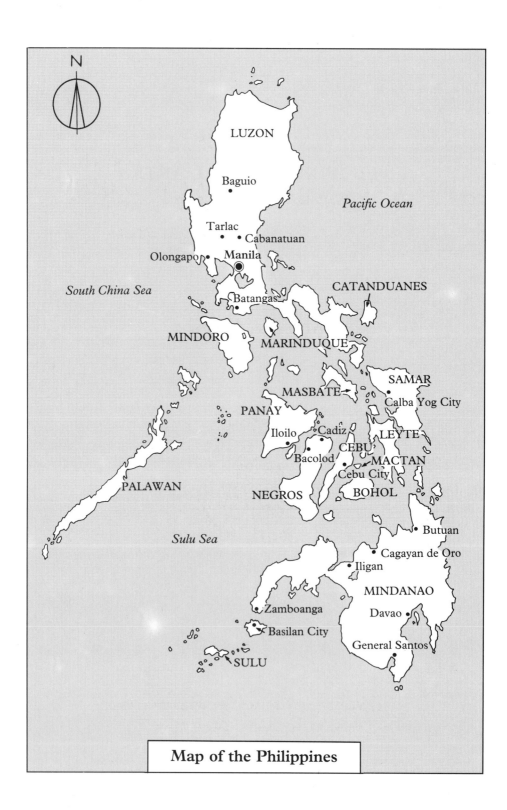

Map of the Philippines

FILIPINO MARTIAL ARTS
Cabales Serrada Escrima

Mark V. Wiley

CHARLES E. TUTTLE COMPANY
Rutland, Vermont & Tokyo, Japan

Disclaimer

Please note that the publisher of this instructional book is NOT RESPONSIBLE in any manner whatsoever for any injury that may result from practicing the techniques and/or following the instructions given within. Since the physical activities described herein may be too strenuous in nature for some readers to engage in safely, *it is essential that a physician be consulted prior to training.*

Published by the Charles E. Tuttle Company, Inc.
of Rutland, Vermont & Tokyo, Japan
with editorial offices at
1-2-6 Suido, Bunkyo-ku, Tokyo 112

LCC Card No. 93-61409
ISBN 0-8048-1913-0

First edition, 1994
Fifth reprinting, 1998

PRINTED IN SINGAPORE

To the memory of Grandmaster Angel Cabales,
whose knowledge, skill, and kindness
are my greatest inspiration.
Through his dedication and integrity,
Escrima is in existence for yet another generation.

▲ Table of Contents ▲

PART THREE: **The Essentials of Escrima Combat**

Note: It is deeply regretted that Grandmaster Cabales passed away during the production of this book. He wrote this Foreword six months before his death.

▲ Foreword ▲

by Grandmaster Angel Cabales
Founder, Cabales Serrada Escrima

For many years I have received proposals from people for writing a book on my style of Escrima. I had turned down all of these offers, feeling uneasy with the idea of my art being available in pictures for anyone to see. However, with the spread of my art as it is going, and my inability to preserve it everywhere, I find it time to document Cabales Serrada Escrima.

I have chosen Mark Wiley, one of my few chosen master instructors, to present my work. I highly recommend this and every book in Mark's collection to anybody who seeks the ultimate, complete documented knowledge of an art. Mark Wiley is, in my opinion, an honest and humble person and a true master in every sense.

▲ Foreword ▲

Contributing Editor, M.A. Training

I have known Mark Wiley for many years now and have watched him grow in the competitive world of the martial arts. I first got to know him years ago while he was in his infant stage of the game, trying to find the ever elusive "secret" of the martial arts.

After many long heart-to-heart talks along with many bone-to-bone bruises and contusions with him, I can now see that Mark found the right path in his pursuit towards martial arts excellence. His dedication to pursue top masters in many areas of the martial arts, from Muay Thai, Wing Chun, Savate, and boxing, to the Filipino martial arts, displays to me that his thirst for knowledge has not yet been quenched. This attribute is the key to achieving greatness in the martial arts.

In this book, Mark has focused on one martial art form, Escrima, and has conveyed the "essence" of the art. I highly recommend this and all of his other books.

▲ Acknowledgments ▲

First and foremost I would like to thank Grandmaster Angel Cabales for sharing his art with me and asking me to write this book.

I would like to thank my parents for giving me the opportunity to begin the study of the martial arts at a young age and to acquire the knowledge that I possess.

I would like to thank Mary J. Hadicke-Wiley, Robert Burns, Sihu Carlos Aldrete, and Master Ian A. Cyrus for taking the time to proofread the original manuscript, Guro David R. Smith for photographing the technique sequences, and Guro Guy Dranoff for posing with me in the photographs.

I would like to also thank those individuals who have offered their suggestions in the writing and presentation of this manuscript: Guro Joe Breidenstein, Guro Fred Degerberg, Master Reynaldo S. Galang, Guro Fred Lazo, Guro Alan McLuckie, Master Darren Tibon, and Guro Mike Young. My research and documentation of the martial arts is inspired by the ground-breaking work of the late Donn F. Draeger and his associates Robert W. Smith and Quintin T. Chambers. Their collective and individual texts have long been trusted reference sources for me and subjects of my admiration.

Many thanks to the Filipino Warrior Arts Association for their perpetuation of Filipino martial culture and sponsorship of Cabales Serrada Escrima.

Finally, I would like to thank the staff of the Charles E. Tuttle Company, their martial arts publications continue to be a step above the rest.

▲ Introduction ▲

Centuries old, the Filipino warrior arts have long been the backbone of Filipino society. It was the practice and preservation of these arts that have kept the Philippine archipelago from permanent domination by a foreign power. There are several hundred styles of these warrior arts presently being preserved and taught throughout the Philippines. Although known by many names, often descriptive of the styles and names of their founders and enemies (i.e., Binas Arnis, Italiana style), the Filipino warrior arts can be classified by three distinct territorial styles—Arnis, Escrima, and Kali—that are found in the northern, central, and southern Philippines, respectively. The purpose of this volume is to introduce the Cabales Serrada system of Escrima in its historical, philosophical, and practical sense. It is important at the outset to make a distinction between the personal style of the system's founder, Grandmaster Angel Cabales, and the collateral systems that are presently being propagated by a number of Grandmaster Cabales' former students.

As is often the case with authentic and traditional martial arts styles, most notably those of Chinese orientation, knowledge is kept from the student until dutifully earned. This occurs without the slightest suspicion on the part of the dedicated student. This method of teaching became the norm because techniques were misused by students, and advanced students proved too often to be disloyal to their instructors. Such was the case too with Grandmaster Angel Cabales.

The entire scope of the Cabales Serrada Escrima system is divided into three distinct segments. Each segment offers more advanced and technically correct methods of movement and application of theories and principles. Grandmaster Cabales' original course of instruction was limited to basic defenses against the system's angles of attack, basic empty-hand techniques, and limited sparring methods. Although. it is unfortunate, many of Grandmaster Cabales' original students were exposed to only one-third of the art. At that time (*circa* 1960), Escrima was relatively unknown other than to Filipinos on the North American continent; therefore, it can be understood why Cabales felt reluctant to openly teach his art, let alone the advanced stages of practice.

In time, Grandmaster Cabales decided to share more advanced techniques and principles with his students. They felt privileged to receive this knowledge, yet these students were made privy to only two-thirds of the system. It was not until his later life that Grandmaster Angel Cabales imparted the remaining one-third of his system. Perhaps because of failing health, Grandmaster Cabales bestowed this final level of knowledge to five of his master instructors.

It is my intention to promote and document the Cabales Serrada system of Escrima in its purest form. I have been doing this through the writing of books and magazine articles, instructional seminars, and training videos. After I had successfully completed my master's training, Grandmaster Cabales encouraged me to do this work, and for that, I am eternally grateful.

The presentation of Cabales Escrima in this book is divided into three parts: history and philosophy, fundamentals of practice, and essentials of combat. Part One describes the history of the Filipino martial arts up to the development of the Cabales system and discusses the philosophy, psychology, and concepts necessary for proper development in this warrior art. Part Two describes and depicts the physical postures and techniques of Grandmaster Cabales' classical Escrima system, and Part Three shows their use in defensive application. Prior to his passing, Grandmaster Angel Cabales read this manuscript, approved it, and wrote its Foreword. He passed away six months after that. Thus, this is the only book that will ever have the full support and endorsement of the founder of the Cabales Serrada Escrima system, Angel Cabales.

—THE AUTHOR

Blackwood, NJ

PART ONE

The History and Philosophy of Escrima

The Cabales Serrada Escrima logo *(overleaf)* is made up of six parts, a *pinute* sword, a stick, a fist, a sun, a triangle, and a circle that surrounds the other five elements. The sword is the primary weapon of the system and all the movements of the stick originated from it. The fist is placed at the bottom because unarmed combat is not emphasized as much as armed combat. The sun, placed at the mind's eye, symbolizes insight. The triangle represents three groupings: the Holy Trinity; Escrima's patterns of defense and offense; and the past, present, and future. It is encircled to show that these concepts are not exclusive but are interrelated.

I

Preliminary Background

*And the sheen of their spears was
like stars on the sea.*
—LORD BYRON

The recording and documentation of history is an arduous and often difficult undertaking. While reading about history we frequently believe the point of view of the author; however, this is often incomplete and inaccurate. In particular, when tracing the origin of an art of war, such as Escrima, it is often difficult to string together the bits and pieces of fragmented information into chronological order. Also, since the exact origin of the art was never documented by those who were directly responsible for its founding, much is left to speculation and the cross-referencing of pertinent information to historical events in the surrounding geographical region.

HISTORY OF ESCRIMA

It has been postulated that the Filipino art of Escrima originated in India and that it was brought to the Philippines by people who traveled through Indonesia across a land bridge known as the Riouw archipelago that linked the Malay peninsula to Sumatra, and across another land bridge that connected Malaya to the Philippine islands. Indonesian Tjakalele and Malay Silat Melayu are two forms of combat said to have been introduced to the Philippines via these now-sunken routes.

The ninth-century Tang dynasty brought goods to the Philippines from East Asia and Malaysia. These countries' combat methods of Kuntao and Silat had a great influence on the development of Kali, which is the "mother art" of the Philippines. Legends claim that ten

21

datus (chieftains) left Borneo and settled in Panay where they established the Bothoan in the twelfth century. The Bothoan was a school where the *datus* taught Kali along with academic subjects and agriculture. It was a kind of preparatory school for tribal leaders.

During the fourteenth century, a third migration of Malaysians to the Philippines took place. These immigrants were the ancestors of the Moro (Muslim) Filipinos of Mindanao and Sulu. They spread their cultural-religious beliefs as well as their Kali systems, which utilized bladed weapons of varying lengths. *Datu* Mangal is credited with bringing the art of Kali to Mactan Island; Sri Bataugong and his son Sri Bantug Lamay were said to have brought the art to the island of Cebu during the Majapahit Empire. Raja Lapu Lapu, the son of *Datu* Mangal, through constant struggle and war, developed a personalized Kali subsystem known as Pangamut. In the sixteenth century, he and Raja Humabon, the son of Sri Bantug Lamay, began to quarrel. A battle was mounting as Lapu Lapu accused Humabon of wrongfully taking land that belonged to his father. The battle, however, was never to take place, as the Philippines were unexpectedly visited by the Portuguese explorer Ferdinand Magellan.

In the early part of the sixteenth century, the Spanish set sail in search of a westward route across the Pacific to the Indies. Commander Ferdinand Magellan's fleet of ships accidentally stumbled upon an unknown archipelago. On March 16, 1521, Magellan came upon the island of Samar. He decided that it was in his best interest to wait to attack, and thus dock at a nearby island. This island was uninhabited and so Magellan's fleet took a few days of needed rest.

On March 18, the Spaniards took note of a boatload of natives coming toward their ships. Commander Magellan, seeing a strategic opportunity, greeted them in friendship. This friendship was to develop, and the native islanders familiarized Magellan with the names of the surrounding islands that made up the archipelago. With the assistance of the ship's priest, Magellan baptized Raja Kolambu, the chief of Samar, and also Raja Humabon, the chief of Cebu, converting them to Catholicism and ultimately to the Spanish allegiance.

On April 27, Magellan led an expedition to nearby Mactan Island in hopes of conquering it and then presenting it as a gift to Raja Humabon. Unfortunately, as he and 49 Spanish conquistadors disembarked from their ships, they were confronted by 1,050 islanders, led by Raja Lapu Lapu, armed with iron-tipped fire-hardened bamboo lances and pointed fire-dried wooden stakes. Greatly outnumbered, Magellan was killed by the spears and arrows of Lapu Lapu's men.

In 1543, Ruy de Villalobos, sailing from New Spain (Mexico), landed south of Mindanao and proceeded to name the entire archipelago the *Philippines* after King Phillip II of Spain. It was not until 1565 that Miguel Lopez de Legazpi, authorized by Phillip II, colonized the island of Cebu, and a foothold was secured in the Philippines. When the Spaniards traveled to the island of Luzon in 1570, they found it inhabited by Filipino, Chinese, and Indonesian cross-cultures, and upon their arrival they were confronted by Kalistas (Kali warriors) whose fighting method far exceeded theirs. But the Spaniards, using firearms, defeated the inhabitants of Luzon. From then on, the art of Kali was prohibited, but it was still practiced and perfected by a dedicated few. The arts were then preserved in native ritual dances called *sinulog* that had mock battles with swords as finales. Ironically, these dances were often performed for the Spaniards' enjoyment.

Kalistas practiced their arts diligently, and hence developed extreme accuracy, speed, and agility. These attributes were a must. Because the Spaniards' swords were sharp and readily cut through the Filipinos' wooden weapons, many strikes to nerve centers along the body and limbs were mastered, allowing the Kalista to disarm and disable his opponent with one strike.

During the 330 years of Spanish reign, after many skirmishes with Spanish fencing exponents and after careful observation, the art of Kali was altered. Many training methods were dropped and many new concepts and techniques were added. This, coupled with the influence of Spanish culture and language, prompted the evolution of Escrima (*a k a* Arnis de Mano). It was the Spanish rapier and dagger systems that had the greatest influence on the development of Escrima. The use of numbered angles of attack as well as what have become traditional Escrima uniforms, were both influenced by the Spanish. It is also interesting to note that although Tagalog is the national language of the Philippines, many of the top Escrima masters still teach their arts in Spanish today.

2

The Evolution of
Serrada Escrima

What is needed is not the will to believe,
but the wish to find out.
—BERTRAND RUSSELL

FELICISIMO DIZON

Filipinos are a proud people, especially in the realm of personal combat. It is a rare practice for one Escrima master to acknowledge the skills of another, let alone speak of him with a tone of respect. There was one man, however, whose name was consistently spoken of in awe. That man was Escrima master Felicisimo Dizon. Master Dizon has been called a "demon" and a "terror" by many expert Escrimadors. His skills, honed through countless death matches, have made him a legend in Escrima circles the world over.

There is a degree of secrecy and uncertainty that surrounds the origin of his art and the master from whom he learned it. Dizon was never one to turn down an opportunity to test his art, and as such was feared by many and respected by all. Dizon, wanting to retain that invincible factor and not wanting others to benefit from the knowledge and skills of his master, was often elusive in discussions of his training. Even among his top students, Master Dizon would often relate varying accounts of the name and location of his teacher and the origin of his art. Through time, however, one such story has been maintained and is now the accepted legend of De Cuerdas Escrima, the art of Felicisimo Dizon. At a young age, Dizon wanted to study under one of the greatest exponents of Escrima, a hermit who lived in a secluded cave. In order to reach the hermit, Felicisimo had to courageously climb a steep mountain cliff. Upon reaching the top, he had to dive into a shark-infested lagoon, and then swim through an underground cavern to the hermit's dwelling. This was done to prove his loyalty to the master.

Dizon learned from the hermit the De Cuerdas style of Escrima, which originated in Cebu. As Felicisimo's ability improved, he wanted to "try out" other renowned Escrimadors. In those days, "try out" literally meant a fight to the death.

Master Dizon never turned down a challenge. He held his art and skills in such esteem that he made no game of De Cuerdas Escrima and would fight for nothing less than the death of one or both participants (these death matches have since been prohibited). There is a story that has been made popular in recent history about a Moro prince who was said to have defeated Dizon, but was later defeated by Dizon's friend and Kali legend, Floro Villabrille. Research has shown that this event did not, in fact, take place. The Moro prince was said to have challenged Dizon to a friendly match to see whose skill was greater. The Moro prince was said to have defeated Dizon, who later asked Villabrille to fight the prince to save his honor. Because Master Dizon never fought for sport, it is unlikely that he would have lost to this Moro, let alone accepted a friendly challenge. If Dizon were to have truly lost, he would not have been alive to continue to teach his art into the 1970s. It is postulated that since Dizon was already an established fighter, Villabrille was looking to build a name for himself and as such invented this story after the death of Dizon in an attempt to further establish his credibility.

Because of Felicisimo's skill in Escrima, he was admitted into the honored Doce Pares Society. This was a society made up of the elite practitioners of the Filipino warrior arts. The final test of the Doce Pares Society was what later came to be known as the "De Cuerdas" tunnel (named after Dizon's fighting style). The tunnel was void of light and sound, and its walls consisted of an array of hardwood sticks and sharp steel blades. The floor was rigged with foot levers that were triggered by pressure. As the Escrimador advanced through the tunnel, he would inevitably step on one of the levers and release one of the weapons from the wall, which would strike out at him. Before entering, an Escrimador's family would have a coffin prepared and waiting for him in the event that he was unsuccessful. Dizon, too, had his coffin prepared, as he honestly thought that he would not succeed in emerging from this tunnel alive.

In spite of this, he was able to exit from the tunnel uninjured. He was the only master in the Doce Pares Society ever to do so. Dizon attributed this success to employing a stick that was considerably shorter than those of the other masters, thus requiring less space to effectively execute his defensive techniques. Master Dizon was said to have possessed *anting-anting* (supreme power through amulets) and after his emergence from the De Cuerdas tunnel, many believed this. In fact, as Dizon was a merchant marine, he would often employ his *anting-anting* to heal the ills of people he came across on his journeys.

In his later life, Master Felicisimo Dizon suffered a number of strokes that left him confined to a chair. He died of a severe heart attack in the early 1970s.

ANGEL CABALES

On October 4, 1917, the course of the Filipino warrior arts was forever changed. On that day in Antique, Panay, Angel Cabales was born. Angel Cabales (Fig. 1), who eventually became a student of Felicisimo Dizon, is the crucial link between the classical art of Escrima and the modern world. Life for Angel began with a series of bad turns. Two weeks after his baptism, his mother, Marta Oniana, passed away. Upon hearing the news of his wife's death, Melcher Cabales went crazy, sold his slaughterhouse, and moved to Mindoro Island, abandoning his three sons Vincent, Canuto, and Angel.

Angel and his brothers were lucky because their aunt and uncle took them in and raised them as their own. Cabales' aunt was a midwife and she took on the sole responsibility of raising Angel and his brothers after her husband's subsequent sudden death. The four of them were fortunate for they never lacked food or shelter. During the farming off-seasons, Cabales' aunt would lend what extra money she had to local rice farmers and in turn she would receive rice from them during harvest times.

Throughout his childhood Angel dreamed of becoming a professional boxer. One day in 1932, when Angel was 15, he witnessed some of the barrio's young men fighting with sticks. Curiosity aroused, Cabales learned that they were in fact practicing an ancient warrior art called De Cuerdas Escrima that was taught to them by Master Felicisimo Dizon. After four months of proving his loyalty to Dizon, Angel was accepted as a personal student. Realizing that he was more suited to stick fighting than boxing, Cabales immersed himself fully in his newfound obsession, De Cuerdas Escrima.

At age 17, Cabales opted for the more exciting life of the big city. Going alone, he packed his bag and traveled to Manila. The first year was tough for him as he tried to survive by working various odd jobs. Angel Cabales had no formal academic education; he claimed his wisdom came from the streets. Then in 1937, Cabales gained good

1. Grandmaster Angel Cabales

work experience working as a foreman for the Madrigal Cement Factory in Rizal, a district near Manila. Cabales worked there for one year then moved back to Manila. At that time he had no trouble finding work and life became easier for him.

To his surprise, Cabales met up with Dizon again while working the Manila docks. Dizon found Cabales' warrior spirit to be strong and taught him the more advanced stages of the De Cuerdas style.

After a hard day's work, the two men would frequent the many local bars. In those days, girls, rice wine, and trouble came easy. It was then that Cabales and Dizon fought in a number of their death matches. Through these experiences, Cabales, like Dizon, learned to appreciate the highly practical aspects of Escrima. Because of their reputations as formidable fighters, they were feared by many, and were thus hired as members of a secret police force that patrolled Manila's crime-infested docks.

Tired of the violence and attracted by stories of wealth and prosperity overseas, in 1939 Cabales, along with members of his "Escrimador gang," became seamen aboard the cargo ship SS *San Jose*. This vessel traveled to many ports around the world, including various places along the coastal United States.

As seafaring adventures usually dictate, these were not relaxing times. Long hours of labor with little money or food left an air of restlessness about the ship. Cabales and his friends often found themselves pitted against other "gangs" they came across on their journeys. Many of Cabales' friends were killed. Aboard the ship, Cabales became involved in an altercation that led to the coining of his system's slogan, "three strikes and a man will fall." One day he was approached by a man claiming to be an Escrimador and was asked if he would like to "practice." He already knew what to expect because in those days, the word "practice," like "try out," meant a duel to the death. Without hesitation, Cabales obliged this man and with the third motion of his stick, the man fell and was never to get up.

Leaving a life of danger aboard the SS *San Jose*, Cabales jumped ship off the coast of California. Upon coming ashore, he found a temporary home in a small Filipino community in San Francisco. In 1945, no doubt in search of further adventure, he traveled north to Alaska and found work in the canneries and fisheries. After a short stay, due to yet another confrontation in which Cabales injured three men, he moved back to California. For the next 20 years, he worked as a foreman in the Stockton asparagus fields.

Life in Stockton was no less eventful. Once again Cabales built his reputation through Escrima. After his arrival, he was asked by many to openly teach his art. Angel initially turned down these requests feeling uneasy with the idea of teaching others how to counter the very skills that had kept him alive. In time, however, he reluctantly agreed. Since there never was a training structure, Cabales set out to standardize the De Cuerdas style to make it easier for the public to comprehend and learn. For the next 20 years, Cabales taught a select few at his home in Stockton, California, while searching for the best means of presenting this art to the public.

In 1965, Max Sarmiento (Figs. 2, 3), Angel's friend, student, and business partner, urged Cabales on, telling him that the future of Escrima rested in his hands. In 1966, Angel Cabales opened the first public Filipino martial arts academy in the United States, earning him the title "Father of Escrima on the Mainland USA."

DEVELOPMENT OF THE SYSTEM

A first step in organizing his system was a standardized ranking structure. Cabales felt that it was necessary to have several levels of students, so he based his rankings on the core of the system, the theory and use of the Twelve Angles of attack. Each angle represented a level of achievement for the student and introduced new material. After the fifth level, Cabales taught various drills for the enhancement of one's reflexes and coordination. Through a drill known as the Lock and

2, 3. Grandmaster Cabales with Max Sarmiento

Block, where a student armed with a single stick defended against an opponent aggressively attacking with a stick and dagger, and by defending against multiple strikes, reflexes and coordination were improved. Through sparring, the techniques were refined and reflexes further developed.

With the attainment of the tenth level, the student was taught the fundamental use of the empty hands for blocking, striking, grappling, and disarming. The empty-hand system was nonexistent in the original De Cuerdas style, but it was something that Cabales felt was a necessary and integral part of any self-defense art.

Since he had extensively altered and added to the De Cuerdas style, Cabales felt a new name was appropriate. It was at that time that

Cabales coined the term *serrada,* meaning "close range" or "to close" (on an opponent) to describe this new standardized system.

As enrollment grew in the Cabales Escrima Academy, Angel realized that a distinction was needed between the skill levels of his instructors. He decided that after a student had passed all twelve levels, he would award him a basic instructorship in Escrima. When a student reached this level, he was responsible for knowing three defenses against each of the system's Twelve Angles of attack, basic disarming, and empty-hand techniques.

The next step, the Advanced Degree, indicated that the instructor was proficient in at least nine single-stick defenses against each of the angles of attack, had a knowledge of advanced sparring principles, including "picking" (faking maneuvers), and was able to reverse any counters to his attacks.

The transition to the Master's Degree was an arduous one. The Master's Degree was mentally and physically the most difficult level to attain. In order to achieve the final level of instruction from Grandmaster Cabales and be considered an expert of Escrima, every movement of the techniques had to be perfect, there had to be mastery over the triangular structure of footwork, the single stick, stick and dagger, disarming, kicking, empty-hand, and sparring techniques. When Cabales tested an instructor at this level, the instructor had to be able to flawlessly reverse all of Cabales' reversals. This is the highest level of the physical art; having the ability to counter an attack and then counter the attacker's reversal of your counter.

LEGACY OF THE GRANDMASTER

During the last 25 years of his life, Grandmaster Cabales had taught literally thousands of people versed in a multitude of martial styles. He had given annual demonstrations and exhibitions throughout California and much of the United States. During the 1970s Cabales made two instructional films for Koinonia Productions. He also made an appearance in the movie *Tiger's Revenge* demonstrating the art of Escrima.

With all of these students and his exposure, why is it that Grandmaster Cabales had only promoted 16 people to the master's rank? The answer: the integrity he felt for his art. Although some accused Cabales of "selling" rank diplomas and "giving" them away after only a weekend of study, they failed to see the whole picture. It is true that many did receive Cabales' advanced diploma after only four days, however these students were given approximately ten hours per day of intensive private instruction directly from Grandmaster Cabales. During such instruction, Cabales would spend hours correcting minute particulars and nuances of the system's movements. Also, these very students had been longtime devotees of Escrima and had trained for years under one of Angel's master graduates. The arrangement was for the master graduates to train their students up to the Advanced Degree, then those students were to go to Stockton for private instruction and testing under Cabales. These were not students who had picked up an Escrima stick for the first time.

During the last three years of his life, Cabales' health began to desert him. With open-heart surgery behind him, he had fought the odds, disregarding the doctor's orders, and continuing to teach a packed schedule of private students and bi-weekly classes at his Stockton-based academy.

Cabales frequently entertained students from out of state wishing to learn directly from the last of the great Escrimadors. He also taught seminars throughout the United States. In his later years, for health reasons coupled with responsibilities on the home front, he tapered his seminar schedule.

In September, 1990, Grandmaster Cabales was admitted to the hospital ravaged by walking pneumonia. What the doctors found however, after a series of tests were run, was a cancerous tumor in his right lung. After three months of chemotherapy, which proved to be ineffective, cancer was also detected in his liver.

Grandmaster Cabales then turned his academy over to his son Vincent. As Cabales' health deteriorated, more and more people began to come out of the woodwork looking for rank and certification under him. It was to Cabales' credit, however, that despite his need for financial stability and the need to feed his wife and two young children, he turned down bribes well into the thousands of dollars.

He later suffered a severe heart attack, and on March 3, 1991, at 11:15 a.m., Grandmaster Angel Cabales passed away. He left this world having led the impeccable life of an Escrimador.

Grandmaster Angel Cabales had certainly done more than his share of promoting and spreading the martial arts of the Philippines. His abilities were so profound and his system so dynamic and effective that such experts as Dan Inosanto, Richard Bustillo, Alfredo Bandalan, Fred Degerberg, Leo Fong, Rene Latosa, Graciela Casillas, and many, many others had sought out his instruction. In 1991 Grandmaster Cabales was posthumously inducted into the Black Belt Hall of Fame as Weapons Instructor of the Year. During the 24 years that Angel Cabales had publicly taught the art of Escrima, more than two thousand people had passed through the doors of his Stockton Escrima academy. It is truly amazing, in a world of exploitation and self-proclamation, that Grandmaster Cabales had never lost sight of his ideals or compromised rank for political reasons. Forty-nine years after his arrival in the United States, Grandmaster Cabales had only promoted 16 instructors to the rank of Master's Degree. It is the quality of his master graduates that gives credibility to his system, not the quantity.

3

Filipino Cultural Beliefs

Test all things and hold fast
to that which is true.
—ST. PAUL

There is a shroud of enigma and mysticism that surrounds the warrior arts of the Philippines. The art of Kali, as taught in the ancient Bothoan, was said to consist of 12 areas of study that included academic and spiritual training in its curriculum. Through the passing down of legends the Filipinos have become a superstitious people that looks to many things for guidance and/or protection. It must be noted, however, that these cultural belief systems provide the Kalista, or Escrimador, with his stable mind and focused intention when engaged in battle. These spiritual beliefs, however, cannot be readily proved true or false. Their successful outcome in combat, although largely dependent on the depth of their user's faith in them, is affected most by the skill level of the fighters.

THE SPIRITUAL BELIEFS

Anting-anting

An *anting-anting* is a charm or amulet made from stone (although it may be of many designs). An *anting-anting* is considered a means of protection from danger as well as something that can distract or confuse an opponent. This confusion gives the owner the opportunity to strike an enemy at will. Most notably, this amulet is said to protect its possessor from being cut by an opponent's sword upon impact. An *anting-anting* is worn on the Escrimador's body, usually around his neck, and is often accompanied by a prayer called an *oracion*.

33

Oracion

Oracions are prayers, usually in Latin, that when chanted, spoken, or mentally recited, serve to protect or strengthen. They may protect one from certain ill fate while traveling in unknown territory, or add strength or additional power to an *anting-anting*.

During the Spanish domination of the Philippines, these prayers were preserved by tattooing them on an exponent's body. These prayers were usually written in the ancient Filipino *alibata* script that is thought to have originated from Sanskrit.

It is believed that for *oracions* to truly work, one must "inherit" them from a family member or close instructor. If you ask for them, buy them from somebody, or read them in a book, they will be of no use and will not work.

Juramentado

The *juramentado* is an oath or vow taken by the Moros of Sulu, based on the Muslim holy wars called jihad. According to the Koran, the jihad was a war waged on Christians and other non-believers of the Islamic faith. Although the purpose, as with most wars, was the death of the enemy, the Koran states (in Surah, VIII, 39) that before a Muslim may kill, he must offer his victims the choice of conversion to the Islamic faith or death.

The act of "running *juramentado*" as practiced in Mindanao, in the southern Philippines, is a corruption of its predecessor. A Filipino Moro would say his prayer, tie an *anting-anting* around his waist (for protection from the "enemy," no less), and proceed to run through the streets with his sword, killing anybody in his path. The belief was that the more people he killed during the *juramentado*, the better his seat in heaven would be.

THEIR RELEVANCE IN SERRADA ESCRIMA

The *anting-anting*, *oracion*, and *juramentado* continue to be a strong part of the warrior arts of the southern Philippines in particular. These cultural belief systems have not wavered over time due to the fact that Mindanao was never conquered or ruled by the Spanish. The Serrada Escrima system, born from De Cuerdas Escrima, holds its origins in the central Philippines, a place that was ruled and affected culturally and religiously by the Spanish invaders for over three hundred years. As a result, the system of Grandmaster Cabales is largely influenced by the Spanish fencing systems and is based on the moral belief system found in the Holy Bible; Cabales himself was a Catholic. Felicisimo Dizon, as stated earlier, was said to have possessed a strong *anting-anting*. It would figure that since Dizon was Cabales' instructor, Cabales should have inherited or at least held a belief in such things. He did not. When asked about *anting-anting*, Cabales stated, "I fight a lot of guys who claim to have *anting-anting*. They claim I cannot hurt them. But, when I slap them right away with my stick and they fall, I know they got nothing." On the other hand, Cabales held a strong belief in the *oracion*. He had a number of Christ figures hanging on the walls of his home and prayed to God regularly. He did not so much pray for protection against an adversary (he had extreme confidence in his physical ability) but rather did it to show his love and loyalty to the Creator.

When I questioned him about the *juramentado* he laughed and warned, "If you see a Muslim wearing white and a turban, and he has his sword resting on his right shoulder, don't walk to his left side or he will turn and cut off your head."

Although these cultural beliefs are not overt in Cabales Serrada Escrima per se, they do appear in various covert forms. For instance, Grandmaster Cabales did wear a red *putong* (bandanna) around his temples. The *putong* is said to be a symbol of bravery among men who had killed several opponents in combat. The color red suggests royalty or authority in the Filipino warrior arts. The actual act of "running *juramentado*" is not practiced by masters of this system; however, the same faith in technique and an unbending will when engaged in combat is prevalent. The fighting spirit of the *juramentado* is developed through intense sparring with weapons. This element of danger is what develops the edge in combat.

4

Psychological Attributes

I come into the fields and
spacious places of my memory,
where are treasures of countless images
of things of every manor.
—ST. AUGUSTINE

AWARENESS

At the outset of any physical confrontation, it is imperative that you be acutely aware of your surroundings and your opponent. You must also be aware of and accept the fact that at the onset of a fight your body will go through a physiological change. During the moments prior to the commencement of combat, your mind will be working much the same as it is right now. Immediately after the conflict begins, however, you will be unable to think, or worry, about what or who is behind you or if your opponent is armed. These things must be determined by a "pre-combat" mind. It is because of this that the Escrimador trains his visual awareness to take notice of minute details and trains his physical skills on the assumption that he will be defending against multiple opponents at all times. Once you engage an opponent, you will be hard pressed to think about anything; you will become intently focused on the destruction of your foe and inherent reactions will have taken over, dictating your responses. Your visual and auditory awareness will slow down to stop-frame. Your mind or thought process, depending on how it has been developed, will speed up.

What has been termed tunnel vision is an area that the Escrimador must learn to accept and keep under control. When involved in a physical confrontation for the first time, many people pick a focal point and everything outside of that point becomes fuzzy. Although having an unwavering focal point seems like a good idea, it is not. Putting all of your attention on one area (e.g., an attacking arm, chest, head) may increase your chances of successfully defending against or attacking that area, but it will decrease your awareness of your surroundings. The Cabales Serrada Escrima exponent understands that there is a good possibility that he may be forced into confronting multiple opponents, so he develops his peripheral vision through the practice of the Lock and Block drill.

Often, for those experiencing an actual fight for the first couple of times, their tunnel vision gets so bad that it decreases to a point no bigger than the size of a man's head and they become unaware of anything happening outside of this focal point. This happens because their minds are not used to and are hence unable to deal with the unexpected rush of adrenaline and fear of the situation. The practitioners of Serrada Escrima look to lessen the apparent threat of the unknowns of combat through realistic sparring with weapons and empty-hand defenses against them. Through these sparring sessions, the Escrimador experiences simulated combat that is in many ways more threatening than an actual confrontation.

By training with weapons, and making physical contact with those of your opponent, you will develop emotional intensity and greater spiritual willingness to take on and accept any challenge, in combat or life. These qualities are manifested through Escrima training because if you miscalculate a strike and miss a block, you will be struck by your opponent's weapon. You must also have the willpower, bravery, and faith in your techniques to walk into an opponent's furious attack, facing certain injury if your technique fails. This type of training opens the door to the development of one's psychological attributes.

MOTIVATION

Motivation is a basic component in the study of any discipline; it is what leads you toward the achievement of your individual goals. You must objectively consider what it is that motivates you toward achieving success in the martial arts. Are you motivated because of quantitative or qualitative incentives, such as money or status? On the other hand, you may be motivated because of the fear of failure in a physical confrontation. Your mental outlook on your training, which is rooted in motivation, will determine your individual behavior both in the training school and outside of it. When you are motivated, you become directed and focused and can therefore clarify in your mind what your individual motives are for obtaining proficiency in Escrima. Once you have achieved this clarity you must set specific long and short-term goals for yourself without expecting immediate results in other areas beyond those that are realistically attainable at that time.

IMAGERY

Imagery, often referred to as visualization or the mind's eye, is the most important form of nonphysical training. Unfortunately, these mental representations are frequently distracted by internal dialogue. Only with the development of discipline will the internal dialogue cease, allowing the dominance of visual symbolism. Once opened, your mind's eye is able to mentally reconstruct visual schemes of your performance of pertinent Escrima movements. Use of visual imagery will actually have an effect on your motor memory and your physical skill.

After developing the discipline to remove unwanted visual symbols, you can then focus your attention on the creative process. During creative imagery, you mentally construct ideal postures, movements, and feelings in your mind's eye and interweave them with those of your actual ability. These ideal postures and movements can come from your memory, photos in books, or videos. This is like placing a piece of paper over a drawing and tracing its lines. Initially your traced creation will appear less than perfect, but in time you will become proficient in its reproduction. However, it is essential that you repeatedly practice your basics in order to physically apply the movements you have worked on during an imagery session.

EMOTIONAL CONTROL

Emotional control is another attribute that an Escrimador must deal with, especially during a physical confrontation. Only when you have control over your emotions will you develop in a proper and efficient manner. Your ability to perform is determined by your degree of self-control when placed in a stressful situation.

Relaxation is a fundamental method of controlling the stress-related feelings that cause anxiety. Anxiety is detrimental to your ability to perform in a given moment. The most important attribute for a martial artist is to be able to perform in the moment. You must have a calm state of mind and be free from tension. If your body is tense, it must first relax before it can initiate a technique, thus lengthening reaction time. Relaxation exercises can assist you in controlling your emotions when in an anxious state. Some relaxation exercises include taking long and deep breaths, meditation, listening to soothing music, and various stretching exercises. As you mature during your pursuit of knowledge and become proficient in Escrima, greater self-discipline, self-esteem, and self-confidence will result. The vast physical, emotional, and mental improvements Escrima training gives you will enable you to better handle the world's unpredictability.

5

Concepts Needed for Practice

Learning is an ornament in prosperity,
a refuge in adversity.
—PAUL KLEE

PROGRESSIONS IN TRAINING

This book concerns the fundamentals of Cabales Serrada Escrima. These basics should not be skipped over for they are the building blocks of an effective combat system. Mastery of the fundamental concepts is a must in order to progress in an effective and efficient manner. All of the advanced principles and techniques are based on the premise that you have a strong foundation and working knowledge of the basics.

After a foundation is built, the Escrima student is taught to execute and defend against the Twelve Angles of attack. After Angle Five has been perfected, reflex development is introduced, and then disarming techniques. Once this has been learned, Grandmaster Cabales' empty-hand system is introduced. The empty-hand system will be ineffective if one does not have the knowledge of zoning, footwork, and distancing taught in the basic weapon movements.

Traditionally, the martial arts of the Philippines are taught in reverse order to those of other countries in that the skills in weaponry are taught prior to those of the empty hand. This is a norm that was developed out of necessity.

The Philippines has always been a warring archipelago. Therefore, an advanced system of armed combat was needed to deter the invasions of armed forces. Escrima is a weapons-based art that was developed by trial and error while fighting unwelcome invaders who wielded sharp swords, and later firearms.

The concept of one-upmanship was understood and practiced by the Filipinos. If an opponent threatens you with a knife, you defend with two knives. If you are attacked with a stick and dagger, you defend with two sticks, or with a dagger and a staff. Because of this concept, unarmed combat was not initially emphasized. However, if the Escrimador was without a weapon, he could easily translate the weapon movements into effective empty-hand techniques.

The need to train with weapons to the same extent, is not a necessity in modern times, though many still believe in this method of training. By training with weapons you are, in fact, developing the attributes necessary for effective empty-hand self-defense.

THE PATH OF PROFICIENCY

To become proficient in any skill takes dedication, hard work, and an unbending desire. Time and dedication to practice are the main ingredients in achieving greatness in Escrima. There is simply no substitute for putting in the long hours of earnest practice; actually it is not the number of hours you put into your training, but the results that you get out of each one that counts. There are absolutely no shortcuts toward attaining proficiency other than years of dedicated, quality practice time. The path of proficiency is a long and arduous one, but the fruits of your labor will be more than compensation.

Repetition is a key factor in any skill that requires a high degree of coordination. A good way to practice Escrima is to repeatedly perform all the footwork, strikes, and techniques while facing a mirror. In this manner, you can see where your mistakes are and if the correct body positions and coverage are present. Another way to develop perfection in techniques is to break them down into their respective parts (e.g., wrist movement, hip rotation, breath control, torque, speed, power). By repeatedly performing each individual movement in a sequence, the sequence as a whole will greatly improve. Mastery requires dedication because only repetition breeds proficiency. By repeatedly doing something it becomes anchored in the body and is something that cannot be taken away or destroyed.

I once asked Grandmaster Cabales why he never did left-handed stick-work; he always held a stick or sword in his right hand and a dagger in his left. "It is more important to be one hundred percent prepared to defend against an attack," he answered, "than to only have fifty percent proficiency on two sides." Cabales continued, saying that an Escrimador's right and left hands have their respective jobs and to train them to perform with unbeatable precision is what wins a fight;

having only half-proficiency on two sides would be useless if you were up against an experienced opponent.

I understand his point of view and can attest to it's effectiveness, having sparred him many times only to effectively land a handful of blows in exchanges of over forty. However, in our modern world, death matches are not as common as in the past. Training from a combative standpoint, Grandmaster Cabales' theory cannot be contested; training from a holistic and artistic standpoint, ambidexterity is a must.

Tennis players and baseball pitchers often suffer from a spinal disorder from the over-development of certain muscle groups on one side of their body. This is also the case with practitioners of Escrima who do not train for ambidexterity. As a bodybuilder lifts weights to develop evenly distributed muscle groups for a well-balanced body, so must the martial artist strive for a symmetrically perfect body. Therefore, developing proficiency on both your right and left sides may hamper your ability to perform in a death match, but the health benefits far outweigh the chances of most martial artists ever being in one.

By training hard in the basics and following the progressions in this book, a good understanding and skill in the art of Serrada Escrima can be gained. To progress to a higher level, you must go beyond the written word and seek a qualified instructor. The key to unlocking personal talent and skill is to be willing to question what it is that you are learning. By questioning, I do not necessarily mean doubting, but rather an intellectual approach to finding permutations of already existing techniques and concepts. Innovation is your best teacher, because it can teach you many things that you subconsciously knew but never physically performed. Work hard and spar with many people of different weapon and empty-hand systems. In this way, you will experience firsthand how Serrada Escrima can work for you.

In learning the fundamentals of Escrima, you will make some mistakes along the way, but, in time, you will evolve from a novice who could not manipulate a weapon to an advanced exponent. The study of any discipline involves various degrees of change. In Escrima, through acquiring the skills of self-defense, that change results in a positive influence on behavior. While learning these techniques one also learns respect and philosophy, making one more humble and centered both spiritually and emotionally. Train hard and true and always be honest with yourself about your level of proficiency. A warrior never holds pretense about his own ability because he knows that his art will never fail him if he trains with dedication, honesty, and integrity.

High and low points during the course of your training will always exist, but with the perseverance to work through those hard times, you will reap the many benefits of understanding the art as well as yourself. Remember, a warrior has nothing to prove to others. It is the process of training that leads to mastery, not the striving for the outcome.

ESCRIMA AS AN ART AND SCIENCE

Serrada Escrima, like all other practices, is an art form. It is the knowledge and understanding of a skill. It is reacting and performing under the stress of an emotional or physical confrontation. For hundreds of years, Escrimadors have improved their abilities by applying their organized knowledge about combat, and it is this knowledge that constitutes a science. Thus, Serrada Escrima as physically practiced and taught is an art; the organized knowledge underlying its practice may be referred to as a science.

As science evolves, so should art. In Serrada Escrima, as in other martial arts, practitioners learn from trial and error. There is no place to turn for guidance other than to one's *guro* (instructor) and the knowledge that lies within. The scientific approach of Serrada Escrima is based on clear concepts, theories, and principles that Grandmaster Angel Cabales developed from experimentation and analysis of the physical movements of the De Cuerdas style. Thus, it is up to the next generation of Cabales Serrada Escrima master instructors to keep the evolution process alive without abandoning the established concepts, theories, and principles that form the nucleus of the system.

There is much to be said about Cabales Serrada Escrima. Your training begins with the interweaving of independent movements. When they reach their apex, the movements become clear, sharp, and unbroken. In this way it reaches its conclusive stage. You must immerse yourself in the art. Intellectualize the art. Digest and become the art. Only then will you come to transcend the art.

PART TWO

The Fundamentals of Practice

The Arsenal of
Serrada Escrima

But, above all, it is most conducive
to the greatness of empire
for a nation to profess the skill of arms
as its principal glory and most honourable employ.
—FRANCIS BACON

When considering the traditional teachings of the various Filipino warrior arts, one will find 12 categories of study. These categories include, but are not limited to, edged, impact, anatomical, projectile, and flexible weapons, both long and short. The various Filipino healing arts, such as Hilot, must also be studied by the Escrimador in order to attain a true understanding and mastery of the art. The effectiveness and beauty of the Cabales system of Escrima rests in its exclusion of wasteful movement and unnecessary training methods. Although there traditionally existed 12 areas of study, many of them were found to overlap and are excluded in many modern Filipino systems. For example, stick and dagger training is fundamentally identical to the double sword if you strike with the stick where the sword would slash.

Serrrada Escrima is merely concerned with the acute development of the single stick or sword, the sword and dagger, empty hand, and the single dagger. Proper development of these four areas of study gives the Serrrada Escrima stylist the ability to successfully defend against double swords, spears, chains, and most other non-projectile weapons. Furthermore, since all weapons are interchangeable (Escrima's claim to fame), the Serrrada Escrima exponent has the ability to translate stick or empty-hand movements into effective sword and shield techniques if the need should arise.

ANATOMICAL WEAPONS

Contrary to popular belief, Escrima is not only an art of stick fighting. Rather, it encompasses the full spectrum of personal combat. Besides the weapons training that is prevalent in most of the martial arts from the Philippines, Escrima makes use of a wide range of empty-hand techniques, including strikes, joint locks, takedowns, and kicks.

Dagger Hand *(Tagang Kamay)*

The dagger hand position is so-called because when assumed, the hand resembles an Escrima dagger. In many martial arts, this hand position is called the knife hand or spear hand. Proper formation includes the extension of the fingers, tightly pressed against one another, with the thumb bent in toward the palm. The dagger hand is used in blocking by moving the arm in the chamber position for the Angle One strike without finishing the attack, for chopping strikes along Angles One and Two, and for thrusting finger strikes along Angles Four and Ten (for more information on the Twelve Angles of attack, see Chapter 8). The chopping technique along Angle Two is particularly effective for striking an opponent in the neck after you have put him into a joint lock.

C-hand *(Ipit Kamay)*

Holding a dual existence, the C-hand is so-called because of its appearance and its clamping action (it is also called the clamp-hand). To form the C-hand, assume the position of the dagger hand, slightly bend your fingers with your forefinger bent slightly more than the others. The Escrima exponent uses the C-hand in two basic ways: as a tool in checking and monitoring an opponent's weapon, and as an aid in joint locking through its clamping action.

Fist *(Suntok)*

The formation of the Escrima fist is identical to the norm in that all the fingers of the hand are tightly clenched with the thumb placed along their side. In Escrima, the fist assumes many shapes, such as the vertical fist, horizontal fist, hammerfist, and the backfist. The desired striking target dictates the type of fist that will be employed. The horizontal fist is most effective when executed along the path of Angles Three, Six, and Eleven, the hammerfist along Angles One, Two, Three, Four, and Eight, and the backfist along Angle Two.

Forearm *(Bisig)*

Escrima uses the forearm not only for blocking but also for striking and disarming. It has three striking surfaces (i.e., the bony edges on each side and the inside of the forearm), and it is an ideal lever that is used in joint locks, disarms, and takedowns.

Knee *(Tuhod)*

In close-quarter situations, the knee is of vital importance to the Escrimador. It is usually used to strike the thigh and chest, and as a lever for displacing an opponent's balance in preparation for a takedown. Knee strikes are often executed along the path of Angles Nine and Eleven. Like kicks, knee strikes are often used after a joint or body lock. The ability to strike with the knee while in motion is trained through the raising of the foot during the Angle Four and Twelve attacking sequences.

Foot *(Paa)*

Not only is the foot a tool for kicking but it is also a primary constituent in the stability of a proper stance. The placement of the foot is vital while stepping and doing takedowns. Proper foot placement and striking during motion is trained through the execution of the classical Twelve Angles of attack.

The kicking techniques *(sipa)* of Serrada Escrima are all executed below one's own waistline. That is not to say that you cannot kick someone in the head, but you must first throw him to the ground, get him in a joint lock, or kick his legs and knees until he falls. Fast low kicks may also be used to distract an opponent. Escrima kicking techniques are kept low so as not to off-balance the Escrimador while engaged in armed combat. Kicking high may also lead to having one's leg cut off. Like all other unarmed techniques, they are incidental and not a central part of the system.

THE ESCRIMA STICK

The single Escrima stick *(solo baston)* is the primary tool used in developing the fundamental skills in the art of Cabales Escrima. It is the first of four categories of training and is the foundation from which advanced training and concepts are built.

Materials

Escrima sticks can be made from just about any material: commonly, rattan, *kamagong* and *bahi*. The most widely used material is rattan

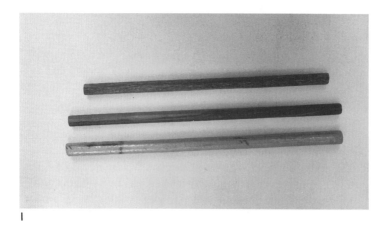

1

2

because it is relatively inexpensive and more accessible than the others (Fig. 1).

Unlike hardwoods, rattan will not chip while training, which decreases the chance of an eye injury; rattan merely frays and gets soft through the course of training.

Rattan is a vine that is grown in various countries, such as the Philippines, China, and Indonesia. Some types of rattan are denser than others resulting in a heavier stick. Since rattan is a vine, it naturally comes with an outer coating or skin. Many Escrimadors prefer that the skin be removed and the vine sanded, although this promotes an accelerated rate of deterioration.

Finding the Proper Length

The length of the stick is generally between 21 and 24 inches. The proper length needed for each individual is found by measuring the distance from your armpit to your wrist (Fig. 2).

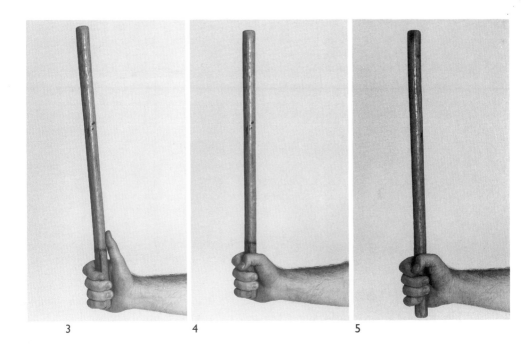

3   4   5

Since Escrima is a close-range fighting system and utilizes many retracting and twirling strikes, a short stick is more economical. One can choose to use a longer stick; however, in close quarters it is harder to manipulate and the chances of hitting your own body with it are greatly increased.

Gripping the Stick

When gripping the Escrima stick, you do not want to have an extremely tight grasp nor too lax a one. The proper amount of force needed to effectively hold and manipulate the stick is the median between too tight and too loose.

At certain times, the thumb may be placed along the side of the stick while blocking for reinforcement (Fig. 3). When striking, all of the fingers must be wrapped along the base of the stick (Fig. 4).

There should be very little, if any, *punyo* (butt-end) showing past the little finger of the grasping hand (Fig. 5). With a long stick, an elongated *punyo* would promote better leverage and allow close-range fighting maneuvers. Since the system utilizes a short stick, this added leverage is not necessary.

6

THE SWORD AND DAGGER

Ultimately a sword-and-dagger (*espada y daga*) system, Escrima initially trains with a rattan stick because it is the most forgiving of its weapons; the stick may break a bone or cause a concussion, but a sword will sever an arm or penetrate the body. Banned during the Spanish occupation of the Philippines, sword and dagger training survived through clandestine training. However, it should be remembered that all of the system's *baston* techniques hold their origin in the *espada* movements; all of the empty-hand techniques come from the *daga*. Thus, although introduced after the stick and empty hand, the sword and dagger (Fig. 6) have, in essence, been practiced since the beginning.

The Espada

The *bolo*, a type of sword, is a common tool often seen hanging from the waist of Filipino farmers. In the Philippines, the *bolo* is often used for gardening, building, or digging. It is no surprise that the *bolo* became the weapon of choice among the Filipino warrior arts, since it was the closest to the individual during a physical confrontation. Serrada Escrima's choice *bolo* is of the *pinute* design. This is one of literally hundreds of sword designs employed by Escrima exponents. The *pinute bolo* is best suited for the system because of its length, weight, and stability. The term *pinute* derives from the word *puti*, which means "white." The sword is so-called because when properly sharpened and held lengthwise toward a light, one should see a white stripe on the sharp edge of its blade.

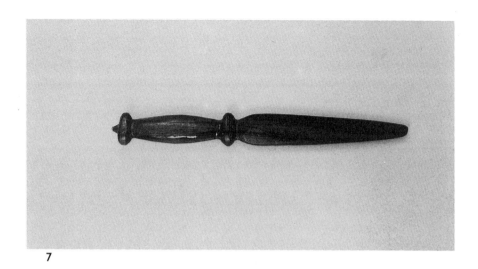

7

The Daga

The *daga*, or dagger, can be of virtually any length up to 18 inches. The design is often identical to that of the *espada* when the two are used together. When used alone or with a stick, the dagger's design is of no significance. A wooden replica is often used during practice sessions for safety (Fig. 7).

7

The Foundation of
Serrada Escrima

I find the great thing in this world is
not so much where we stand,
as in what direction we are moving.
—OLIVER WENDELL HOLMES

This is the first chapter that deals with physical instruction. The information in the preceding chapter is the basis of all Cabales Serrada Escrima techniques. Without understanding the proper body positioning, the concept of distance, essential footwork, striking qualities, proper body mechanics, and the Alive Hand, any techniques learned would be inadequate. There would be no foundation from which to build, no substance behind the blocks and strikes, and consequently no structure. As a result, freedom of expression through movement would not exist.

BODY POSITIONS

Traditionally there were 33 postures taught in De Cuerdas Escrima. These postures included, but were not limited to, methods of holding your weapon while walking down a crowded street, how to sit on your stick allowing for quick access if necessary, and how to stand with your stick, in an unassuming manner, with both of your hands free for use. These positions were essential for the survival of an Escrimador in the Philippines at the time of their conception. Because many of them are no longer practical or useful in modern times, only a handful of them are retained in the Cabales Serrada Escrima system. These postures are presented below.

1   2

The Natural Position *(Tindig Luwagan)*

This posture is assumed while standing in the Escrima class line or when talking to another student or instructor. Stand with your legs a shoulders' width apart, feet pointing forward, stick under your left bicep with your left hand grabbing your right forearm (Fig. 1).

The Attention Position *(Tindig Paggalang)*

This posture is assumed at the beginning and end of each training session, when receiving instruction from the *guro* and while awaiting an opponent's strike during training. Your feet should be a shoulders' width apart and your stick and free hand by their respective sides (Fig. 2).

3   4

The Courtesy Salutation *(Bigay Galang)*

The salutation is a sign of respect that is given to your *guro*, seniors, and training partners. Starting from the ready position (Fig. 3), put your weight on your left foot, and step back and across with your right foot. As this is being done, raise your weapon, placing the point at the center of your forehead while placing your left hand on your navel (Fig. 4).

The Ready Position *(Tindig Serrada)*

This is the position that the exponent assumes when preparing to spar or fight. This is a variation of the Angle Two attack position. Stand with your right side forward and your torso turned slightly to the left. The left hand is placed in front of your navel. The right hand, holding the stick, is placed over the heart with the stick in the crook of your left elbow (Fig. 5).

5

6

The Lock and Block Position *(Laban Tayong)*

This position is never held statically; rather it is a combative ready position where the effect of inertia has already been overcome by the constant motion of the hands. The locked position is held between defensive counters while waiting for the next attack. Standing with your right side forward, keep your left hand over the stick, moving them back and forth in short lateral motions (Fig. 6).

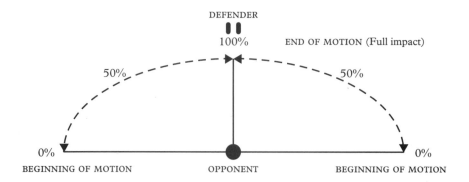

Zoning Diagram

FOOTWORK

The core of the offensive and defensive movements is the knowledge of zoning and the skills in movement through footwork. There are two safety zones and two types of footwork employed in Cabales Serrada Escrima.

Zoning *(Pook)*

Zoning refers to movements made with the intention of effectively blocking or evading an opponent's strike. There are two reference points, at the beginning and at the end of a given motion.

If someone were to strike you, his maximal force would be aimed at a specified area; for example, your face. At the points just before and just after the desired point of impact, there is considerably less force. This is because you have to build up the force needed to accelerate your weapon, and after the point of impact it is necessary to slow down to halt the momentum of your strike.

It can be very dangerous to attempt to block a strike at its point of full impact. It is best to either jam the strike before it has built up its full force (Fig. 7), or pass the weapon and employ a check during its retraction (Figs. 8, 9).

7

8

9

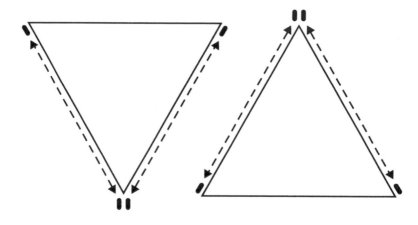

Forward Triangle   Reverse Triangle

Triangle Stepping *(Hakbang Tatsulock)*

The footwork patterns taught in the Serrada system are based on the triangle. There are both forward and reverse triangles as shown above. The forward triangle is generally used for defensive purposes and the reverse triangle is generally used in offensive movements.

There are three points to a triangle: a frontal location, known as the point of the triangle, and two rear locations known as the base of the triangle. When fighting, one generally places his stick or strong side on the point of the triangle, and steps to either base of the triangle to initiate both offensive and defensive techniques.

Replacement Stepping *(Salit-salit)*

Replacement stepping is the core of the defensive movements because in Escrima one never steps back or retreats, instead one employs body shifting and zoning. When defending attacks to the left side of your body, it is better to have your right side forward, and vice versa. You can defend against an attack to your right with your right side forward if the timing does not allow replacement stepping; however, it is stronger and much safer to zone. This type of footwork is called replacement stepping because you are replacing the front foot with the rear foot. Although this is also triangle stepping, I have made this distinction in order to emphasize its importance in defense.

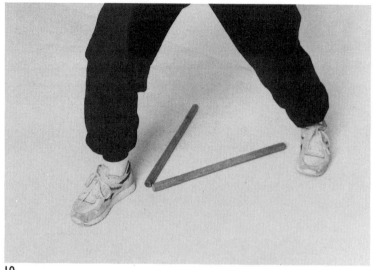

10

11

12

To do this, stand with your right foot at the point of the triangle and with your left foot at the left base corner (Fig. 10). Move your left foot to the point of the triangle (Fig. 11). As it meets your right foot, move your right foot to the right base corner of the triangle (Fig. 12). This can be done on both the right and left sides, and as many times as is necessary in your defense.

13

14

THE CONCEPT OF DISTANCE

A critical distance can be defined as any distance that has the ability to form a crisis or threatening situation. In Escrima that refers to any distance from which your opponent can strike you with his edged, impact, or anatomical weapons. There are four distances in Serrada Escrima, three of which are critical. Offensive as well as defensive strategies must be understood, developed, and mastered in each of the four ranges. The concept of distancing must be understood because there is no set numerical distance between each range. The critical distance of each range is determined by the height of the opponent and length of the weapons.

Distancia de Fuera

This is a distance at which neither you nor your opponent can strike one another with a weapon (Fig. 13), or with the empty hand (Fig. 14).

15

16

This range allows you to briefly study or "feel out" your opponent. Although often held for only a brief moment, every confrontation must pass through this "probing" range for you to be in the correct distance to strike your opponent.

Distancia Larga Mano

Larga mano, meaning "long hand," represents the farthest distance at which you can strike or be struck by your opponent. It is a range at which your opponent cannot strike you with his weapon (Fig. 15), but you can strike your opponent's hand with yours (Fig. 16). In this range, your offensive and defensive techniques become one. Your defensive block, in turn, becomes your offensive strike, and vice versa.

17

18

Distancia Medio

This is a medium range at which most of Serrada Escrima's techniques come into play. It is at this distance that you and your opponent are given the opportunity to strike one another in the head (Fig. 17). Because of this danger, the Alive (left) Hand is introduced (Fig. 18). The majority of disarming techniques are also executed in the *medio* range.

19

20

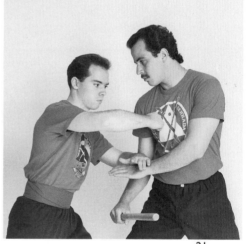

21

Distancia Corto

Corto, meaning "close" or "short," is the closest range that is encoun-
tered while standing. In this range, you are a bit too close to execute
many of the actual striking techniques. Consequently, the Escrima
stylist drops his weapon and continues the altercation unarmed (Figs.
19–21). The empty-hand system taught in the Serrada Escrima system
is most effective in this range.

22   23

STRIKING QUALITIES

It is important to understand how to strike an opponent in a variety of ways and how to defend against such attacks as well. If only one method of striking existed, then there would be no need for self-defense because everyone would know what to expect. Serrada Escrimadors utilize a variety of offensive techniques to effectively strike an opponent. They also have a broad knowledge of various striking permutations that consequently allows them to successfully defend against such strikes.

Primero

This is the first striking method. It is executed with force, and stops at the point of impact and is held (Figs. 22, 23). This method of striking is never done in combat because it would be too easy for your opponent

24   25   26

to strike or even cut off your arm. Leaving your arm in any given position is leaving it prone to your opponent's attack. The *primero* strike is used for training purposes, however. By striking and holding the strike at the point of impact, you are allowing your training partner to practice the correct form and positions for defending against a full-powered strike.

Lobtik

This is a full-powered strike that is aimed through a desired target. This method of striking does not retract or stop at the point of impact; rather it follows its path from beginning to end (Figs. 24–26). This strike does not stop until it comes to the end of its motion, unless it is met with resistance or is blocked.

27   28   29

Witik

This method of striking involves retraction, which is useful when switching directions or angles of attack. The strike is initiated in the same manner as the *primero* strike however at the point of impact, it retracts, making it more difficult to block, check, or disarm (Figs. 27–29). This type of strike is the most popular among Serrada Escrimadors because of its speed and the uncertainty of where the next strike will come from. Faking maneuvers and multiple striking are all executed in the *witik* form.

30

31

32

Abaniko

The *abaniko* strike is a fanning motion that is made with the stick (Figs. 30–32). It is a *witik* strike that switches angles of attack. The *abaniko* can be executed horizontally, diagonally, or vertically. It is important that the body and arms move in sync to provide the proper mechanics needed for a powerful whipping motion. Many times an *abaniko* strike is utilized to fake or set up your opponent, enabling you to pick your desired target area (hence "picking" is the term used to describe faking techniques).

33   34   35

36

Arko

This is the twirling motion of the stick that is seen in many of the basic Serrada stick counter sequences. The stick is twirled in either an upward or a downward motion (Figs. 33–35). An important but often overlooked error is the releasing of the fingers while twirling (Fig. 36). Do not release your fingers while twirling the stick. Although the looser grip may initially appear to aid your speed, the power and stability of the strike are greatly decreased. Relax your hand but keep your fingers grasping the stick. With perseverance and proper training, you can perform this motion in the correct manner.

PROPER BODY MECHANICS

Many of the techniques illustrated in this book have been exaggerated so that the reader will be able to better visualize their paths and motions. The techniques must be done quickly and accurately during practical application with as little wasted motion as possible. All of the movements must be condensed and solid.

Any strike that is done with the mere extension of an arm is weak and considerably slower than one that makes use of the whole body as a single functioning unit. A strike that is initiated from just the arm is only as strong as that arm, but a strike that involves the entire body is as strong as the combined elements of that body.

The power of the strikes and blocks is derived through the hips and from stomping. If the hips move first and the body follows, there is considerably more power and force generated than if just the arms are moved.

Theoretically, there are no stances in Escrima. Consequently, elusive footwork is preferred to a still posture. Stability is achieved by stomping the ground with the lead foot. This stomping assures a solid stance upon impact.

One of the objectives in weapons combat is to have the ability to be covered with your extremities protected while in an offensive mode. This can be achieved by gaining an understanding of torque through the proper use of body mechanics.

THE ALIVE HAND *(Bantay Kamay)*

The understanding and use of the Alive Hand is perhaps the single most important quality that a beginning Escrima student must develop. The Alive Hand is typically misunderstood and often disregarded in training. However, developing this skill may very well be the attribute that saves your life.

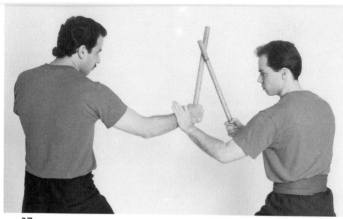

37

38

Explanation

If you were holding a weapon, your empty hand, generally the left, would be considered your Alive Hand. This is the hand that is responsible for the checking of your opponent's hand or the weapon itself (Figs. 37, 38). The Alive Hand is used for disarming, striking, thrusting with a knife, and passing (Figs. 39–42).

39

40

41

42

43   44

Positions

The positioning of the Alive Hand is very important. The hand is always held near the chest until it is time to come into play. The most common hand positions are with the palm facing toward your chest or to the right (Figs. 43, 44). There are many other positions, however the previous two are the most common among Escrimadors today.

It is important not to leave your hand extended in a checked or locked position for a long period of time. If this happens, chances are you may lose it. By keeping the arm extended you are leaving it prone to reversal (Figs. 45–47) or attack (Fig. 48). Your opponent may simply grab it, strike it, or even cut it. There is also a chance that you will accidentally strike your own arm (Fig. 49).

After an attack has been checked or countered, the Alive Hand must return to the chest area where it can be safe and ready for its next move. This way, the hand is kept out of the path of both your own and your opponent's attacks.

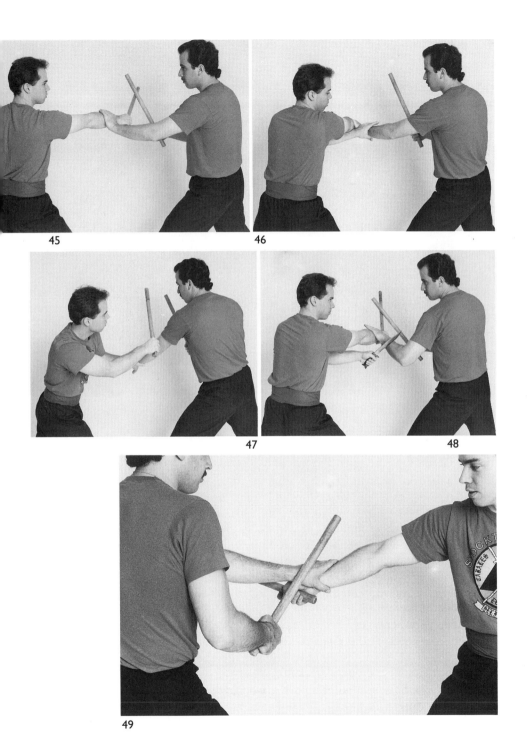

45

46

47

48

49

50

51

52

53

54

Use in Blocking

If an opponent were striking at you and you blocked with your stick and then countered, there is still a possibility that his weapon might strike you (Figs. 50–52). By making use of the Alive Hand, you can momentarily trap or immobilize your opponent's arm, preventing it from continuing along its path after the removal of your initial block and counter (Figs. 53, 54). This allows you to set up an opponent by controlling his attacking arm, thus limiting his options.

PART THREE

The Essentials of Escrima Combat

8

The Twelve Angles of Attack

Invincibility lies in defense,
the possibility of victory in the attack.
—SUN TZU

THEORY AND PURPOSE

In the Cabales Serrada system, various offensive and defensive movements are taught through the use of *abakadas* (angles of attack). These *abakadas* consist of 12 strikes to vital areas on a person's body.

Why defend against angles of attack? The answer is simple. There are a countless number of possible techniques that someone could use to attack you, and to learn specific techniques to defend against each of them would not only be time-consuming but nearly impossible. By training with the angles of attack as opposed to methods of attack, the Escrimador automatically covers all possibilities of defense.

The Angle One strike is delivered to the left side of the head, neck, or collarbone. If someone were to kick you, punch you, or strike you with a stick to the left side of the head, why would you defend against each of them differently? On the surface they may all appear to be different, however, upon closer examination it can be seen that they all move along the same path of movement, aimed at the same target: the left side of your head.

By knowing various defenses against the Angle One strike, you are automatically equipped to defend against any attack moving along that path. There may be slight differences in your zoning or body positioning, but for the most part the defenses would be identical.

79

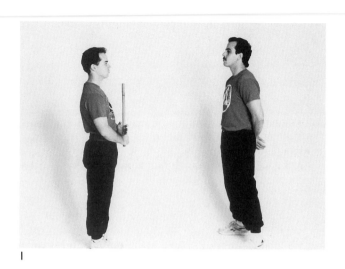

I

THE NUCLEUS OF A SYSTEM

The *abakadas* are executed in a classical sequence to preserve the art form, and in a combative manner to promote effective striking qualities. The Twelve Angles of attack, when classically executed, form the nucleus of the Serrada Escrima system. Although there are no standardized forms, the execution of the classical sequence can be thought of as such. Often viewed as a mere series of movements used to teach striking techniques, the Twelve Angles contain within their structure the entire foundation and all the advanced techniques of the Serrada system, such as footwork, stances and postures, hip and arm movements, striking and slashing techniques, blocking and deflecting techniques, disarms and reversals, punches, strikes, and kicks. If there is ever a doubt as to the proper placement of a stick, block, or hand technique, the answer can be found in this series of movements. Every technique can be proven correct or incorrect by referring back to the movements in the classical execution of the Twelve Angles of attack. This is perhaps the most important area of study. Learn these movements well and practice them diligently.

ANALYSIS OF THE TWELVE ANGLES

Although many systems of Escrima utilize angles of attack, there are no two numbering systems alike. Many systems have similarly numbered angles and often the first five are identical, but the remaining angles are different. The Serrada Escrima attacking system contains eight strikes and seven thrusts. Although this number of techniques equals 15, they

2

3

are executed within the Twelve Angles through combination and simultaneous movements. The following photos illustrate the Twelve Angles of attack as classically executed in the Cabales Serrada system of Escrima.

Angle One: Forehand Strike to Collarbone
(Anggulo Isa: Tagang San Miguel)
From the attention position, cross your stick and hand in front of your chest (Fig. 1). Step back with your right leg, place your right hand over your right chest, and raise your stick vertically in front of your left hand (Fig. 2). As you step forward, strike your opponent's left collarbone (Fig. 3).

4

5

6

Angle Two: Backhand Strike to Collarbone
(Anggulo Dalawa: Bartikal)
From the attention position, raise your right heel off the floor, bend your left arm so that the hand is in front of your navel, and bend your right arm so that the stick is placed diagonally over your left elbow (Fig. 4). As you step forward, strike to your opponent's right collarbone (Figs. 5, 6).

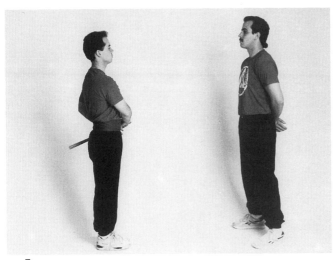

7

8 9

Angle Three: Forehand Strike to Hip
(Anggulo Tatlo: Tabas Talahib)
From the attention position, move the stick to your left hip, placing your left hand over the portion of the stick just behind your right hand (Fig. 7). Step back with your right leg, moving the stick and left hand to your right hip (Fig. 8). As you step forward with your right leg, return your left hand to your chest, striking horizontally to your opponent's left hip (Fig. 9).

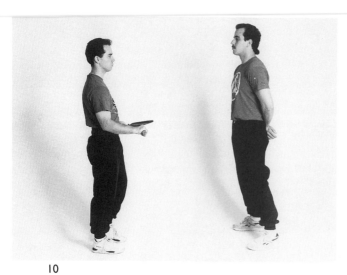

10

11

12

Angle Four: Thrust to Sternum and Backhand Strike to Hip
(Anggulo Apat: Saksak at Tagang Alanganin)

From the attention position, raise your left foot and lift your stick waist-high so that it is parallel to the ground while placing your left hand, holding a dagger, on top of the stick (Fig. 10). As you step forward, leaving the stick in place, thrust the dagger toward your opponent's solar plexus (Fig. 11). As you retract the dagger, deliver a horizontal backhand strike, palm down, to your opponent's right hip (Fig. 12).

13

14   15

Angle Five: Thrust to Stomach
(Anggulo Lima: Saksak sa Sikmura)
From the attention position, move the stick to your left hip, placing your left hand over the portion of the stick just behind your right hand (Fig. 13). Step back with your right leg and raise the stick so it is parallel to the ground and place your left hand, palm down, near the front of the stick (Fig. 14). Stepping forward with your right leg, retract your left hand and thrust the stick to any area between and including the navel and the groin of your opponent (Fig. 15).

16

17   18

Angle Six: Forehand Thrust to Shoulder
(Anggulo Anim: Saksak sa Kanan)

From the attention position, raise the stick horizontally in front of your face with your left hand, palm facing out, on the frontal left side of the stick (Fig. 16). Then step back with your right leg, keeping the stick in place (Fig. 17). As you step forward with your right foot, retract your left hand while delivering a thrust to the left part of your opponent's chest (Fig. 18).

19

20   21

Angle Seven: Backhand Thrust to Shoulder
(Anggulo Pito: Saksak sa Kaliwa)
From the attention position, lift your right heel while raising the stick
horizontally so the butt is in front of the left side of your chest, and place
your left hand, palm facing you, on the stick (Fig. 19). As you step
forward, retract your left hand and deliver a thrust with the stick, palm
up, to the right side of your opponent's chest (Figs. 20, 21).

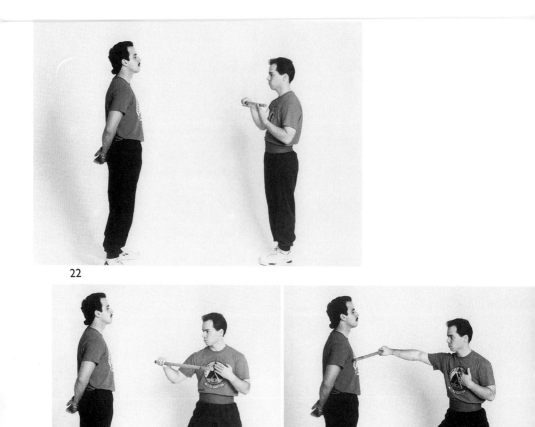

22

23

24

Angle Eight: Backhand Strike to Chest
(Anggulo Walo: Tagang Alanganin)

From the attention position, raise the stick to your chest horizontally so that it is parallel to the ground, and place your left hand, palm facing in, in front of the stick (Fig. 22). As you step forward with your right leg, retract your left hand and make a horizontal slashing strike from the right to the left side of your opponent's chest (Figs. 23, 24).

25

26   27

Angle Nine: Backhand Strike to Knee
(Anggulo Siyam: Aldabis sa Ilalim)
From the attention position, turn to the left while slightly bending both
knees, placing your left hand over the stick and behind the right hand
(Fig. 25). As you step forward, retract your left hand and deliver a strike
diagonally, palm down, from your opponent's right knee to his left
shoulder (Figs. 26, 27).

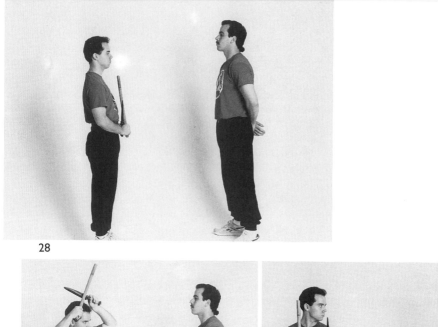

28

29   30

Angle Ten: Thrusts to Chest and Throat
(Anggulo Sampu: Saksak sa Kanan)

From the attention position, cross your stick and dagger in front of your chest (Fig. 28). Step back with your right leg while making an umbrella-shaped motion over your head with your stick and dagger, finishing the motion with both weapons vertical and parallel in front of your chest (Figs. 29, 30). Thrust your dagger into your opponent's chest, raising the stick so it is parallel to the ground (Fig. 31). While twisting your body, deliver a thrust with the stick to your opponent's throat (Fig. 32).

31   32

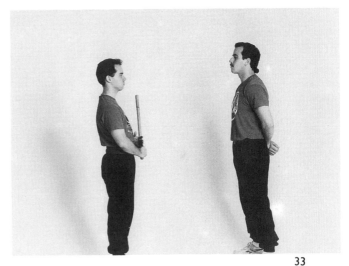

33

Angle Eleven: Forehand Strike to Knee
(Anggulo Labing-Isa: Saboy)
From the attention position, cross your stick and left hand in front of
your chest (Fig. 33). Step back with your right leg while making an

34   35

36

umbrella-shaped motion over your head with your stick and left hand
(Figs. 34, 35). End this motion with your stick touching the ground and
your left hand near your chest (Fig. 36). As you step forward, deliver a
diagonal strike, starting from your opponent's left knee and ending at
his right shoulder (Figs. 37, 38).

37   38

39   40

Angle Twelve: Matador's Thrust

(*Anggulo Labindalawa: Dalawang Bulusok*)

From the attention position, cross your stick and dagger in front of your chest (Fig. 39). Raise your left heel while making an umbrella-shaped motion over your head with your stick and dagger (Figs. 40). End this

41

42

43

44

motion with your stick and dagger parallel and in front of your chest (Figs. 41, 42). Raise the stick and dagger so the tips of both are pointing down (Fig. 43), and step forward with your left foot as you thrust the weapons to each side of your opponent's collarbone (Fig. 44).

9

Basic Stick Defenses

We must train ourselves to regard everything
as a possible weapon and use our imagination
to find techniques that are suitable.
—QUINTIN CHAMBERS

The single stick is the first of four categories that are practiced by exponents of Serrada Escrima. The progression of learning the single stick follows that of the Twelve Angles of attack as discussed in Chapter 8. Proficiency in three single-stick defenses against each of the angles of attack is required, along with other requisites, for one to achieve the rank of *guro*.

This chapter depicts and describes one defense against each of the Twelve Angles of attack, and is used as a vehicle for presenting an overview of Serrada Escrima's single-stick defenses.

COUNTERING THE SINGLE STICK

There are dozens of basic stick counter techniques in Serrada Escrima, but they are simplistic. All defensive sequences follow a simple three-step pattern starting with one of the eight primary defenses *(sangga)*, then one of two follow-up sequences, and ending with what is known as the "Locking Technique." The eight primary defenses consist of six blocks and two passing techniques. Any potential attack can be deflected or passed using one of these eight defenses.

The difference between the two follow-up sequences lies in the initial

95

1   2

defense, which dictates whether to counter an attack on the inside or outside of an opponent's arms.

The final movement of all counter sequences is what is termed the "Locking Technique." It has nothing to do with a joint lock per se, but it acts as a final checking or covering position utilized to end an attack while preparing for another. The Locking Technique consists of three movements: first, a check with the stick to the last position of your opponent's weapon; second, a dagger thrust or strike to an open target; and third, the ready, or Lock and Block Position.

The best way to defend oneself is to be well prepared and to act on instinct without the hesitation caused by a lengthened thought process. Serrada Escrima overcomes this "lag time" by ingraining two basic counter sequences and the Locking Technique into the body through continual repetition. Every possible attack can be nullified using a combination of these blocks, passes, and counters. In advanced Serrada Escrima training, freelanced movements are employed and the need for and theory of prearranged counter sequences is discarded.

Angle One: Cross Block
(Anggulo Isa: Sangga Kruzada)
As your opponent attacks, step straight forward with your right leg (Fig. 1). As his weapon is blocked, your stick will cross his and your left hand will be checking his attacking hand (Fig. 2). Once contact is made, turn your hips to the left, bringing your opponent's arm to your hip, pulling him off-balance (Fig. 3). As you turn to face your opponent, your left hand remains as you strike his forearm (Fig. 4) and pull your stick into your navel so its point faces your opponent (Fig. 5). Using the *arko* motion, strike under your opponent's wrist, check his hand, then strike the top of his wrist (Figs. 6–8). Pull your stick back near your hip as you

3

4

5

6

7

8

9

10

11

utilize your final check (Fig. 9). Finish with the Locking Technique (Figs. 10, 11).

Angle Two: Outside Block
(*Anggulo Dalawa: Sangga sa Labas*)
As your opponent attacks, step forward with your left leg (Fig. 12). As his weapon is blocked, your stick should be in the Angle One chamber position and your left hand should be checking his wrist (Fig. 13). Once contact has been made, slightly push out with your left hand while turning your hips to the left. As your body is in motion, strike the opponent's right arm with your stick (Fig. 14), then flip your stick over to check his arm (Fig. 15). Finish with the Locking Technique (Figs. 16, 17).

18

19

20

21

Angle Three: Two-step Pass
(Anggulo Tatlo: Dalawang Hakbang Pasunod)

As your opponent attacks, take a half step backward with your left leg and chamber your stick (Fig. 18). As the opponent's stick nears your waist, pass it by with your left hand (Figs. 19, 20). As the stick passes, step back with your right leg and counter with an Angle One strike to the opponent's forearm (Fig. 21). Step up to the point of the triangle (see Replacement Stepping, Chapter 7, p. 60) as you check your opponent's arm and follow through with your strike (Fig. 22). Now step back with your left leg as you continue your stick's *arko* motion (Fig. 23). As you complete the replacement stepping, the *arko* motion is also completed, striking your opponent's forearm once again (Fig. 24). Then flip your stick over to check the opponent's arm (Fig. 25), finishing with the Locking Technique (Figs. 26, 27).

22

23

24

25

26

27

28
29
30
31

Angle Four: Flip Block
(Anggulo Apat: Sangga Abaniko)

As your opponent thrusts his dagger (Fig. 28), step back with your right leg, and block the knife (Fig. 29). As the opponent attacks with an Angle Four strike, step up to the point of the triangle, using your left hand to pass the stick and flipping your right wrist to hit the opponent's wrist with your stick (Fig. 30). Complete replacement stepping as you pass his stick and initiate the *arko* motion (Fig. 31). As you complete your footwork, strike the opponent's wrist, check his hand, and strike the top of his wrist (Figs. 32–34). Pull your stick back near your hip as you utilize your final check (Fig. 35). Finish with the Locking Technique (Figs. 36, 37).

32

33

34

35

36

37

38   39

40   41

Angle Five: Cross Block
(Anggulo Lima: Sangga Kruzada)

As your opponent thrusts his stick (Fig. 38), turn your hips to the left, raise your stick waist-high, and place your left hand under your stick. As the opponent's stick nears your groin, step back with your left leg; your stick will intercept the oncoming stick and your hand will be checking the opponent's hand (Fig. 39). As you turn to face your opponent, your left hand remains as you strike his forearm (Fig. 40) and pull your stick into your navel so its point faces him (Fig. 41). Using the *arko* motion, strike under your opponent's wrist, check his hand, and strike the top of his wrist (Figs. 42–44). Pull your stick back near your hip as you utilize your final check (Fig. 45). Finish with the Locking Technique (Figs. 46, 47).

42

43

44

45

46

47

48

49

Angle Six: Outside Block
(Anggulo Anim: Sangga sa Labas)

As your opponent attacks (Fig. 48), step forward at a 45-degree angle with your left leg. Chamber your stick to guard your groin while passing the opponent's stick with your left hand (Fig. 49). Rotate your right wrist and strike your opponent's arm with your stick (Fig. 50). Step back with your right leg as you check your opponent's arm with your left hand (Fig. 51). Then turn your hips to the left as you strike your opponent's wrist with an Angle One strike (Fig. 52), and flip your stick over to check his arm (Fig. 53). Finish with the Locking Technique (Figs. 54, 55).

50

51

52

53

54

55

56

57   58

Angle Seven: Shoulder Block
(Anggulo Pito: Sangga Balikat)
As your opponent thrusts his stick (Fig. 56), step forward with your left leg, and check his right arm with your left hand, raising your stick, point down, to intercept his stick (Figs. 57, 58). Check the opponent's right arm with your left hand as you step back with your right leg (Fig. 59). Turn your hips to the left as you strike the opponent's arm with your stick (Fig. 60). Then flip your stick over to check his arm (Fig. 61). Finish with the Locking Technique (Figs. 62, 63).

108   PART THREE: ESSENTIALS OF ESCRIMA COMBAT

59

60

61

62

63

64

65

66

67

Angle Eight: Punch Block
(Anggulo Walo: Sangga Suntok)

As your opponent strikes (Fig. 64), raise your stick and left arm (behind your stick) up and in front of your chest (Fig. 65). As the stick nears, do a smooth punching motion toward the floor with your hand holding the stick and chop down with your open left hand. Do not drop your stick below your waist (Fig. 66). After contact is made, continue the strike's motion by passing the stick with your left hand as you step back with your left leg (Fig. 67). Using the *arko* motion, strike under your opponent's wrist, check his hand, then strike the top of his wrist (Figs. 68–70). Pull your stick back near your hip as you utilize a final check (Fig. 71). Finish with the Locking Technique (Figs. 72, 73).

68

69

70

71

72

73

74

75

76

77

Angle Nine: Flip Block
(Anggulo Siyam: Sangga Abaniko)

As your opponent strikes (Fig. 74), step back with your left leg, and lift your right leg knee-high. Rotate your right arm to the left, and strike his oncoming wrist with your stick (Fig. 75). Step forward with your right leg while flipping your stick and striking under the opponent's wrist (Figs. 76, 77). Complete the *arko* motion by checking the opponent's arm and striking the top of his wrist (Figs. 78, 79). Bring your stick near your waist, utilizing a final check to his right arm (Fig. 80). Then finish with the Locking Technique (Figs. 81–83).

78

79

80

81

82

83

84

85

86

87

Angle Ten: Inside Block
(Anggulo Sampu: Sangga sa Loob)

As the dagger thrust comes toward you, step back with your right leg and turn your stick outward to block it (Fig. 84). As the opponent thrusts his stick, step back with your left leg and block with your stick (point up) while checking the base of the stick with your left hand (Fig. 85). Retain the checking hand position on the weapon, turn your hips to the right and counter with an Angle Four strike to your opponent's hip (Fig. 86). Turn your hips to the left and strike the underside of the opponent's wrist (Fig. 87). Using the *arko* motion, check the opponent's hand, and strike the top of his wrist (Figs. 88, 89). Pull your stick back near your waist, employing a final check (Fig. 90). Finish with the Locking Technique (Figs. 91–93).

88

89

90

91

92

93

94

95

Angle Eleven: One-step Pass
(Anggulo Labing-Isa: Isang Hakbang Pasunod)
As your opponent strikes, raise your left hand and stick (Fig. 94). As the strike is about to hit you, step back with your left leg as you control the stick's passing with your left hand (Fig. 95). As the opponent's stick passes by, strike his arm with your stick (Fig. 96), and flip your stick over to check his weapon (Fig. 97). Finish with the Locking Technique (Figs. 98, 99).

96

97

98

99

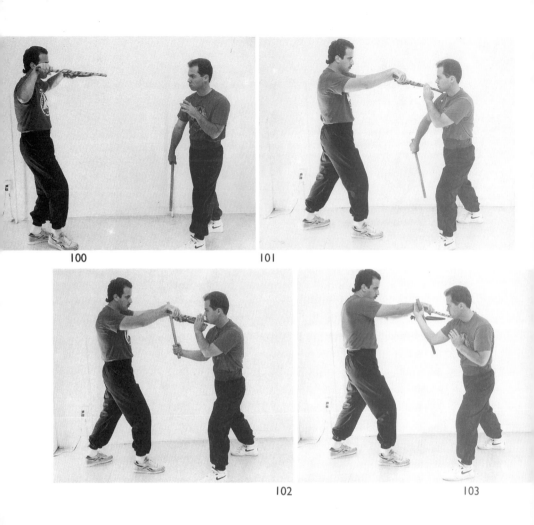

100   101

102   103

Angle Twelve: Outside Block
(Anggulo Labindalawa: Sangga sa Labas)

As your opponent attacks, step forward at a 45-degree angle to the left (Fig. 100). Parry his stick with your left hand (Fig. 101), and strike your opponent's wrist with an outside block strike (Fig. 102). Move your stick to a shoulder block position to the outside of the opponent's right arm (Fig. 103). Check the opponent's right arm with your left hand as you step back with your right leg (Fig. 104, 104'). As you turn your hips to the left, strike the opponent's arm with your stick (Fig. 105), then flip it over to check his arm (Fig. 106). Finish with the Locking Technique (Figs. 107, 108).

104

104' (second view)

105

106

107

108

The Unarmed
Defensive System

The eye of a master,
will do more work than his hand.
—BENJAMIN FRANKLIN

As was discussed earlier, unarmed combat is traditionally the last category of training that is introduced in Escrima. Once the student had mastered this level, he would be considered a true Escrimador (one who is proficient in all categories of Escrima). However, when restructuring of the De Cuerdas Escrima style, Grandmaster Cabales chose to introduce empty-hand training in the middle of the Serrada system. The Cabales Serrada Escrima empty-hand system is made up of four sub-systems, each of which is made up of individual techniques. These four sub-systems are blocking methods, striking methods, joint locks, and body locks. At the outset, the student is taught the techniques of each sub-system individually. After a high degree of proficiency has been attained, each of the individual techniques are combined in such a way as to create one complete system of empty-hand defense. An analysis of the striking methods is outside the scope of this book. This chapter is meant to be a bridge between the single-stick movements of Chapter 9 and the empty-hand disarms of Chapter 11. The empty-hand striking surfaces are described in Chapter 6 allowing the interested reader to analyze the weapon movements and create empty-hand techniques of his own.

Again, as with knowing multiple weapon counters, the knowledge of a multitude of empty-hand blocks, strikes, and locks is essential for

1   2

developing an effective and efficient defense. There are approximately 16 locking techniques in Serrada Escrima. This book will not describe all of them as it is meant to give the reader a basic overview of the Serrada Escrima system. Thus, this chapter is limited to describing and depicting eight methods of locking the joints and body.

BLOCKING METHODS

The empty-hand blocking system is limited to three methods. With these three blocks as a foundation, the Serrada Escrima stylist is encouraged to study and analyze the weapon techniques in order to translate their movements into advanced empty-hand counters. The three primary blocks are discussed below. After they have been learned, the student should practice them in a continuous flowing motion against a series of punches coming from a variety of angles.

Cross Block *(Sangga Kruzada)*
As the opponent initiates an attack (Fig. 1), cross your hands and move them forward to meet the oncoming force (Fig. 2). The choice of whether to place your left or right hand on top is dependent on your last position and the specific application you are applying. The moment

3

your hands make contact with your opponent's, redirect the oncoming force by moving your hands off your center (Fig. 3). The choice of whether to move your hands to the right or left, again, is dependent on your last position and your chosen application. Note that you move your block to the right so that you will be on the outside of your opponent's center. If you turn your block to the left, you would be in between both of your opponent's arms, leaving yourself open to a follow-up strike.

C-hand (*Ipit Kamay*)

As your opponent initiates an attack (Fig. 4), move your arm (that is on the same side as his strike) forward to meet it (Fig. 5). When your hand meets the opponent's wrist, with the use of the C-hand, immediately grab his wrist. Once you have successfully taken control of the oncoming arm, move your hand toward your center, taking the force of his strike and redirecting it (Fig. 6).

Outside Block *(Sangga sa Labas)*

As the opponent initiates an attack (Fig. 7), turn your upper torso toward the direction of the attack. Extend your lead hand to intercept and parry the initial force of the attack (Fig. 8), sending it slightly off its course. Then retract your lead hand and replace it (moving the rear arm under the lead arm) with your rear hand (Fig. 9). As your rear hand makes contact with the opponent's forearm, employ the C-hand and clamp his wrist, taking control of his attacking arm. Regardless of which hand the opponent attacks with, you will always intercept the strike with your lead hand and clamp with the rear.

4

5

6

7

8

9

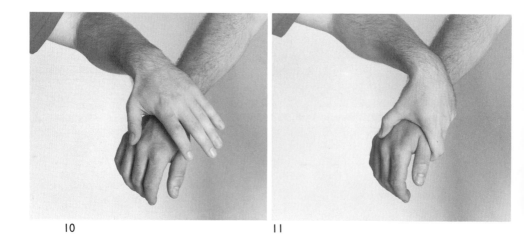

JOINT LOCKS

The act of seizing an opponent's limbs and immobilizing his joints is no easy task. Many martial arts' joint-locking techniques involve grabbing a hand out of the air during an attack. This in itself is highly unlikely, since the oncoming hand is moving much too fast to grab and the opponent is not likely to let you lock his joints without showing a good deal of resistance. The Serrada Escrima exponent realizes this and as such employs methods of blocking and striking to first distract an opponent and weaken his ability to resist. Once applied, these locks can be used to immobilize or break an opponent's limbs, or to disarm him.

There are over a dozen joint-locking techniques *(trankada ng kasukasuan)* involved in the Cabales Serrada Escrima curriculum. In this section I will describe four of the most commonly used joint locks. This section is not concerned with how the defender got to the point of being able to lock an opponent. Not unlike empty-hand striking techniques, joint locks are considered incidental and, as such, one should not consciously try to apply them. You may, in the course of attacking, defending, or disarming, find yourself in such a position as to be able to safely apply a locking technique. It is at this time, and only this time, that you should consider attempting one.

Joint Lock One *(Trankada ng Kasukasuan Isa)*
With your arms in a parallel position, grab your opponent's right hand (Fig. 10). While in this position, your fingers seize the meaty part on the underside of the opponent's thumb while your thumb presses between the bones on the back of the opponent's hand (Fig. 11). Rotate your

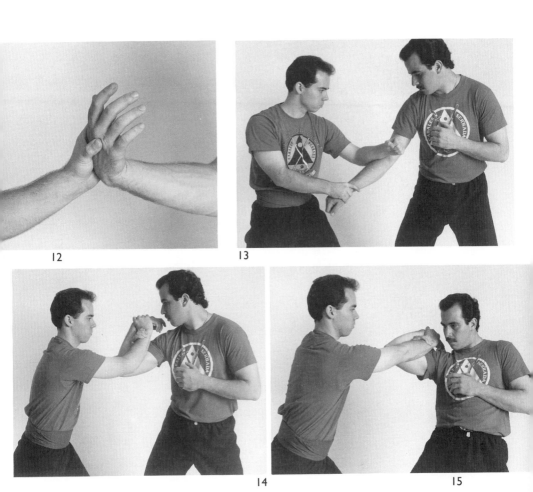

12

13

14

15

hand away from the opponent's center while twisting his wrist (keeping your arm immobile) toward the ground with your thumb (Fig. 12). The direction of the twisting motion is dictated by which hand you are locking. The direction you twist an opponent's wrist will dictate where he will fall.

Joint Lock Two *(Trankada ng Kasukasuan Dalawa)*
From a cross-wrist grab using the C-hand, apply pressure with your left forearm to bend the opponent's elbow (Fig. 13). Keeping your left arm in place, move the opponent's wrist toward his shoulder (Fig. 14). Once in place, grab your right wrist with your left hand and apply pressure past the opponent's shoulder (Fig. 15). You may apply direct pressure that will force the opponent to fall backward, or you may twist the arm to the left, forcing him to fall to the left.

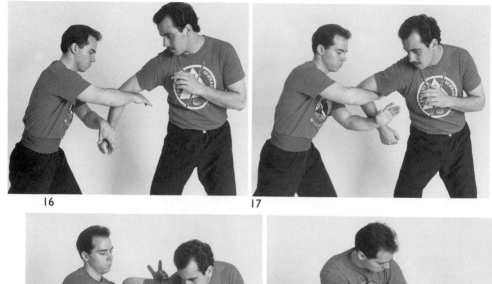

16   17

18   19

Joint Lock Three *(Trankada ng Kasukasuan Tatlo)*
While redirecting the opponent's arm, insert your right arm under his
elbow (Fig. 16). Using a push-pull action (Fig. 17), push the opponent's
hand toward his own chest with your left hand while you pull his elbow
toward your chest with your right hand. Once his arm is sufficiently
bent, slide your left arm in the opening and take hold of his shoulder
(Fig. 18). Once the shoulder is locked, grab your left forearm with your
right hand and pull the opponent toward you and the floor (Fig. 19).

20

21

22

23

Joint Lock Four *(Trankada ng Kasukasuan Apat)*
Redirect the opponent's oncoming strike with the back of your left
hand (your palm is facing you) by drawing an imaginary clockwise
circle (Figs. 20, 21). When your hand completes one full circumfer-
ence, use the C-hand and grab hold of the opponent's wrist (Fig. 22).
Cup your right hand over the extended elbow of your opponent and
apply downward pressure (Fig. 23). It is important that while applying
downward pressure you do not move your left arm. Movement will
reduce the stability and leverage needed to effectively execute the elbow
lock.

24   25

BODY LOCKS

The next level of empty-hand training concerns locking, controlling, or immobilizing an opponent's entire body. It is far more difficult than joint-locking in that it involves controlling an entire body, not just one limb.

Body locks (*trankada ng katawan*) are principally used in the Serrada Escrima system as a means of finishing or ending a confrontation. Timing is essential in the application of necessary entry techniques and defensive postures as you near an opponent. Once the gap has been bridged, the Serrada Escrimador employs one of a number of body locks to immobilize, take down, and eventually finish off his opponent.

Body Lock One *(Trankada ng Katawan Isa)*
As you close the gap on your opponent (Fig. 24), be sure to monitor his arm at all times (Fig. 25). Your right arm crosses over the opponent's right arm as your left hand checks his elbow, preventing him from striking you (Fig. 26). At this point, your right leg should be behind the opponent's legs breaking his balance (Fig. 27). Grab your right wrist with your left hand and take him down (Fig. 28).

Body Lock Two *(Trankada ng Katawan Dalawa)*
As you come into contact with your opponent, direct his attacking arm so that you are defending on the outside of his body (Fig. 29). As you step in with your left leg, keep control of the opponent's arm with your right arm while your left arm strikes his throat on the way to grabbing his left shoulder (Fig. 30). Your left leg is behind the opponent to break his balance while you lock his right elbow and bend your left elbow into the opponent's throat, cutting off his air supply (Fig. 31).

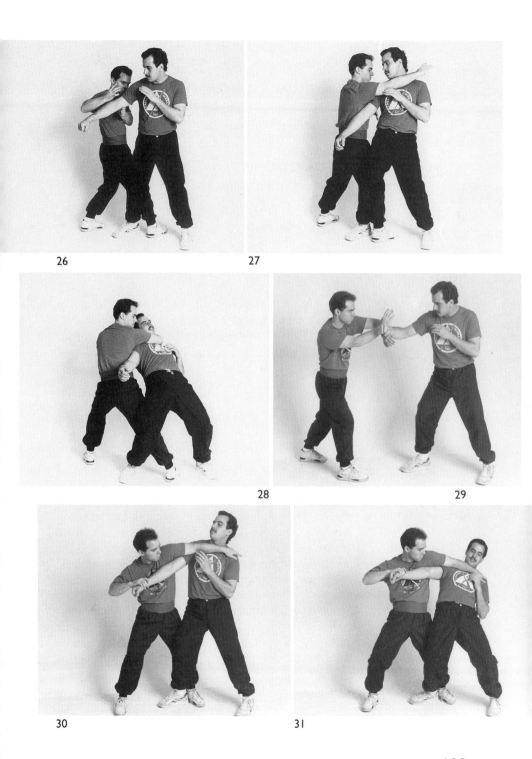

26

27

28

29

30

31

32

33

34

35

Body Lock Three *(Trankada ng Katawan Tatlo)*
In the first cross-body throw your goal was to interrupt an opponent's
air supply. In this lock, you will take him down and finish with a groin
strike. As you come into contact with your opponent's attacking arm
(Fig. 32), employ the chambering motion of Angles Ten, Eleven, or
Twelve while grabbing the wrist, and enter on the inside of the
opponent's arm by stepping in with your left leg (Figs. 33, 34). At this
point, your left leg is behind the opponent to break his balance as your
left hand controls his right shoulder. Finish the technique by taking
your opponent down as you strike his groin with a right hammerfist
(Fig. 35).

36

37

38

39

Body Lock Four *(Trankada ng Katawan Apat)*

As your opponent attacks with a right punch, parry the strike with an outside block (Fig. 36). Using the C-hand, hold his wrist with your right hand (Fig. 37). Take a large step behind your opponent as you bring his arm under his body and through his legs. When his arm is between his legs, switch hands and place your right hand on his neck or upper back as you lift his arm (Figs. 38, 39). This will create a great deal of pain as you throw him to the floor.

Basic Techniques of Disarming

The exponent who is unarmed or disarmed
does not suffer any disadvantage;
he can fight effectively.
—DONN F. DRAEGER

As was discussed in Chapter 3, because of the constant threat of armed attack, initially the empty-hand system of Escrima was not stressed. However, even though there was not a systematic method of learning the empty-hand techniques, if the Escrimador was without his weapon he could easily translate his weapons movements into effective empty-hand techniques. This chapter depicts that translation, showing how the stick counters of Chapter 9 are applied when one is unarmed. This chapter is not, however, concerned with the minute details of disarming methods *(agaw)*, such as proper zoning, alignment of limbs, weapon and body levers, pressure points, pressure sensitivity, and follow-up techniques. Rather it will demonstrate the practical use of weapons training in unarmed defense by showing a direct correlation of weapon to empty-hand movements for each angle of attack.

EMPTY-HAND DISARMS

Angle One Disarm *(Agaw Anggulo Isa)*
As your opponent attacks (Fig. 1), raise both your hands, right crossed above left, and step forward with your right leg. As your foot plants,

1

2

3

4

your left hand should make contact with the stick (Fig. 2). Once contact has been made, immediately turn your waist to your left, redirecting the force of the strike (Fig. 3). Grabbing the stick with your left hand, pull the stick upward while striking down on the opponent's weapon arm with your right wrist (Fig. 4).

5   6

7a   7b

Angle Two Disarm *(Agaw Anggulo Dalawa)*

As the opponent strikes, step forward with your left foot while raising both arms (Fig. 5). As contact is made, your left hand firmly grips your opponent's wrist, and your right hand is held in the Angle One chamber position (Fig. 6). Pull your opponent's thumb off his stick with your left hand as your right forearm begins to apply pressure to the stick (Figs. 7a, 7b). When the thumb is released, thrust your bent right arm toward your opponent, pushing the stick out of his grip (Fig. 8). The stick should strike your opponent during the disarm.

8

9   10

Angle Three Disarm *(Agaw Anggulo Tatlo)*

As your opponent attempts to strike, you raise your left hand waist-high
and your right hand chest-high (Fig. 9). Take a half-step back with your
left foot and control the stick's passing with your left hand (Fig. 10). As

11

12

13

the stick passes your midsection, step back with your right leg as you grab your opponent's wrist with your right hand (Fig. 11). Next, step up to the point of your triangle as you twist the opponent's wrist (Fig. 12). Step back with your left leg while turning the stick clockwise out of your opponent's grip (Fig. 13).

14   15

16   17

Angle Four Disarm *(Agaw Anggulo Apat)*

As the opponent strikes, plant your weight onto your right foot as you prepare to pass the stick with your left hand (Fig. 14). As the stick nears your body, redirect it with the knife-edge of your left hand and grab the opponent's hand with your right hand (Fig. 15). Step back with your right leg and turn the opponent's hand so it is palm up while applying a wrist lock (Fig. 16). Disarm the opponent by turning the stick clockwise out of his grip (Fig. 17).

18   19

20   21

Angle Five Disarm *(Agaw Anggulo Lima)*

As the opponent thrusts with his stick (Fig. 18), step back with your left leg and redirect his attack (Fig. 19). After redirecting the thrust, grab the stick with your left hand (Fig. 20). Next, strike the opponent's wrist with your right forearm as you pull the stick out of his grip with your left hand (Fig. 21).

Angle Six Disarm *(Agaw Anggulo Anim)*

As your opponent thrusts his stick, begin to move on a 45-degree angle to your left (Fig. 22). As the stick comes closer, control its pass with your left hand (Fig. 23) and pull your left hand back while grabbing the opponent's wrist with your right hand (Fig. 24). Step back and across with your right leg so that you are now facing your opponent as you twist his hand so that his palm is facing up (Figs. 25, 25'). With your left hand, turn the stick clockwise to remove it from his grasp (Fig. 26).

22

23

24

25

25' (detail)

26

27   28

Angle Seven Disarm *(Agaw Anggulo Pito)*
As your opponent attempts to thrust (Fig. 27), step forward with your left foot, turning your torso slightly to the right. With your right forearm guiding the thrusting stick, grab his attacking hand with your left hand (Fig. 28). While peeling the opponent's thumb off of the stick, push your bent right arm toward him (Fig. 29), knocking his stick into his own body as you disarm him.

Angle Eight Disarm *(Agaw Anggulo Walo)*
As the stick nears your body, slightly extend your left hand to intercept the strike (Fig. 30). As your left hand makes contact with the stick, drop your weight to redirect the oncoming force (Fig. 31). Grab your opponent's wrist with your right hand while stepping back with your left leg (Fig. 32). Then rotate your left hand, pulling the opponent slightly off-balance while applying a wrist lock (Fig. 33). Once the opponent's arm is hyperextended, peel the stick out of his hand with your left hand, disarming him (Fig. 34).

29

30

31

32

33

34

35

36

37

38

Angle Nine Disarm *(Agaw Anggulo Siyam)*
As the stick nears your knee, step back with your right foot (Fig. 35),
lower your center of gravity, and pass the base of the stick with your left
hand (Fig. 36). As the stick passes your leg, wrap your left hand around
the opponent's attacking wrist, and place your right hand under the
opponent's hand to immobilize it (Fig. 37). Disarm the opponent by
abruptly jerking your left hand to the left, hyperextending his wrist (Fig.
38).

39   40

41   42

Angle Ten Disarm *(Agaw Anggulo Sampu)*

As the lead punch, or dagger thrust, is a quick set-up maneuver, one should only attempt to deflect it (Fig. 39). As the stick thrust nears your throat, turn your torso to the left while executing the cross block deflection with your arms (Fig. 40). As your opponent's hand comes into reach, grab the base of his weapon with your left hand and chamber your right arm for a downward strike (Fig. 41). To disarm your opponent, pull your left hand toward your chest as you apply a sharp downward strike with your right forearm to his wrist (Fig. 42).

43

44

45

46

Angle Eleven Disarm *(Agaw Anggulo Labing-Isa)*

As your opponent steps forward to strike you, step back at a 45-degree angle with your left leg and pass the weapon with your left hand to redirect its force (Fig. 43). Immediately take control of the strike by seizing the opponent's wrist with a right C-hand (Fig. 44) and turning it upward to pull him off balance (Fig. 45). When the opponent's arm is hyperextended, step in with your left leg and peel the stick out of his hand with your left hand while maintaining your right C-hand. Finish by applying an arm bar (Fig. 46).

47

48

49

50

Angle Twelve Disarm *(Agaw Anggulo Labindalawa)*

As your opponent attempts a double thrust (Fig. 47), step forward at a 45-degree angle with your left foot while passing his stick with your left hand and striking his abdomen with a right punch (Fig. 48). Keep contact with the opponent's weapon and rotate your left hand clockwise, grabbing the base of the stick while leaning back with your body and holding the opponent's wrist with a right C-hand (Fig. 49). Disarm the opponent by taking a step back with your left leg and peeling the stick out of his hand (Fig. 50).

▲ Afterword ▲

Although no single text alone is sufficient for one's development in a martial art, it is my hope that this volume has given you an idea of the background, development, and foundation of the Serrada Escrima system of Grandmaster Angel Cabales. Although this volume covers a great deal of the Serrada Escrima system, it is in no way meant to be a substitute for a qualified instructor, whose instruction is essential for proper development in this warrior art.

I now leave you with a popular saying of Grandmaster Cabales. When asked about combatting styles that make use of sticks 30 inches and longer, he said, "I don't care if you got a mile-long stick, I'll block it with 18 inches." No art must be viewed as better or worse than all others, just different. As there are different tastes for different people, so are there different martial arts. Your ability to perform in combat is rooted in the confidence and faith you have in your art. Grandmaster Angel Cabales was the epitome of such qualities.

Mabuhay ang Escrima
(Long Live Escrima)

Lineage of Cabales Serrada Escrima

There is no doubt that many will claim authority in the Escrima of Angel Cabales; however, there is no room for controversy. Listed below are the certified masters of Cabales Serrada Escrima under the late Grandmaster Angel Cabales.

DIPLOMA NUMBER	RECIPIENT
1	Johnny Cabales
2	Vincent Cabales
3	Jimmy Tacosa
4	Jaime Cabrera
5	Lee Foster
6	Ronnie Saturno
7	Kimball Joyce
8	Wade Williams
9	Frank Rillamas
10	Gabriel Asuncion
11	Darren Tibon
12	Jerry Preciado
13	Khalid Khan
14	Mark V. Wiley
15	Rey Tap
17	Charles E. Cadell, III

Author's Note: This lineage was given to me by Grandmaster Cabales upon graduation from his Cabales Escrima Academy. There were actually 17 diplomas to have been filled out by him, however one of the advanced instructors had not completed his master's training prior to Grandmaster Cabales' death. Certificate 16 was therefore never officially awarded or recognized.

Glossary of Filipino Terms

abakadas: the angles of attack
abaniko: a fanning strike
agaw: a disarming technique
aldabis sa ilalim: a backhand strike to the knee (Angle Nine)
anggulo: any one of the angles of attack
anim: the number six
anting-anting: an amulet or charm of supernatural power
apat: the number four
arko: a twirling motion of the stick
Arnis de Mano: (lit., armor of the hands) a fencing art developed in the
    Philippines

bahi: a tree with a grain that looks like the scales of a snake
balikat: the shoulder
bantay kamay: the Alive Hand
bartikal: a backhand strike to the collarbone (Angle Two)
baston: a cane or stick used in Escrima, Arnis, and Kali
bigay galang: the courtesy salutation
bisig: the forearm
bolo: a type of machete used in Escrima
Bothoan: a secret, ancient school of weaponry

daga: a dagger or knife used in Escrima
dalawa: the number two
dalawang bulusok: the matador's thrust (Angle Twelve)
dalawang hakbang pasunod: a two-step pass defense
datu: chieftain
distancia corto: close range
distancia de fuera: outside or pre-contact range
distancia larga mano: long range

distancia medio: medium range
doble: a double movement in a sequence

Escrima: a fencing art developed in the Philippines
Escrimador: a master of Escrima
espada: a sword used in Escrima
espada y daga: the sword and dagger used in Escrima

guro: an instructor of Filipino martial arts

hakbang tatsulock: triangle stepping

ipit kamay: the C-hand
isa: the number one
isang hakbang pasunod: a one-step pass defense

juramentado: the ancient Moro act of running amok

Kali: An ancient Filipino warrior art named after the *Kali* sword
Kalista: a master of Kali
kamagong: a dark wood extracted from the Narra tree
katawan: the body

laban tayong: the lock and block position
labindalawa: the number 12
labing-isa: the number 11
lima: the number five
lobtik: a strike that follows through its target

Mabuhay ang Escrima: Long Live Escrima

oracion: a prayer

paa: the foot
Pangamut: Raja Lapu Lapu's personal subsystem of Kali
pinute: a type of Filipino sword or machete known for its balance and durability, usually double-edged near the tip
pito: the number seven
pook: zoning
primero: the first category of striking, taught for training purposes
punyo: the butt of an Escrima stick
putong: a headband worn as a symbol of bravery by Escrimadors who have killed several opponents in combat

saboy: a forehand strike to the knee (Angle Eleven)

saksak at tagang alanganin: a thrust to the sternum and backhand strike to the hip (Angle Four)

saksak sa kaliwa: a backhand thrust to the shoulder (Angle Seven)

saksak sa kanan: a forehand thrust to the shoulder or thrusts to the chest and throat (Angles Six and Ten)

saksak sa sikmura: a thrust to the stomach (Angle Five)

salit-salit: replacement stepping

saludo: a salutation or sign of respect used in Escrima

sampu: the number ten

sangga: a defensive technique

sangga abaniko: a flip block or fanning block

sangga balikat: a shoulder block

sangga kruzada: a cross block

sangga sa labas: a block to the outside

sangga sa loob: a block to the inside

sangga suntok: a punch block

Serrada: (lit., close range) the Escrima system of Angel Cabales

sinulog: a native Filipino ritual dance that had a mock battle with swords as a finale, used to secretly preserve Escrima and Kali techniques during the Spanish occupation

sipa: a kick

siyam: the number nine

solo: a single motion or the use of a single weapon

sumbrada: (lit., shadow) a method of weapons sparring using an even number of counter techniques and offensive strikes

sumgob: a finger thrust

suntok: a punch

tabas talahib: a forehand strike to the hip (Angle Three)

tagang alanganin: a backhand strike to the chest (Angle Eight)

tagang kamay: the dagger hand

tagang san miguel: a forehand strike to the collarbone (Angle One)

tatlo: the number three

tindig luwagan: the natural position

tindig paggalang: the attention position

tindig serrada: the ready position

trankada: a locking technique

trankada ng kasukasuan: a joint-locking technique

trankada ng katawan: a body-locking technique

tuhod: a knee or knee strike

walo: the number eight

witik: a retracting strike